JAM
ON

LAENA McCARTHY

PHOTOGRAPHY BY
MICHAEL HARLAN TURKELL

JAM ON

THE CRAFT OF CANNING FRUIT

VIKING STUDIO

VIKING STUDIO
Published by the Penguin Group
Penguin Group (USA) Inc., 375 Hudson Street,
New York, New York 10014, U.S.A.
Penguin Group (Canada), 90 Eglinton Avenue East, Suite 700,
Toronto, Ontario, Canada M4P 2Y3
(a division of Pearson Penguin Canada Inc.)
Penguin Books Ltd, 80 Strand, London WC2R 0RL, England
Penguin Ireland, 25 St. Stephen's Green, Dublin 2, Ireland
(a division of Penguin Books Ltd)
Penguin Books Australia Ltd, 250 Camberwell Road, Camberwell,
Victoria 3124, Australia
(a division of Pearson Australia Group Pty Ltd)
Penguin Books India Pvt Ltd, 11 Community Centre, Panchsheel Park,
New Delhi – 110 017, India
Penguin Group (NZ), 67 Apollo Drive, Rosedale, Auckland 0632,
New Zealand (a division of Pearson New Zealand Ltd)
Penguin Books (South Africa) (Pty) Ltd, 24 Sturdee Avenue,
Rosebank, Johannesburg 2196, South Africa

Penguin Books Ltd, Registered Offices:
80 Strand, London WC2R 0RL, England

First published in 2012 by Viking Studio,
a member of Penguin Group (USA) Inc.

1 3 5 7 9 10 8 6 4 2

Copyright © Laena McCarthy, 2012
Photographs copyright © Michael Harlan Turkell, 2012
All rights reserved

ISBN 978-0-670-02617-3

Printed in the United States of America
Set in Janson Text LT Std
Designed by Renato Stanisic

*For my friends and cosmic family, who nourish with food,
laughter, art, music, and joy*

Taken at Brooklyn Grange rooftop farm

CONT

ENTS

I

LAENA'S STORY

Hanging off the beam of my forklift in the middle of winter in Antarctica, trying desperately to kick the frozen forks open as the wind bore down on me across the frozen ocean, I would have laughed incredulously had someone told me that five years later I would be running my own jam and jelly business in New York City. But that's just where I ended up. I went from working on a remote research station with the United States Antarctic Program to starting my own preserved fruit manufacturing company a few years later. Life is strange and miraculous.

I began making jam in my early twenties, when I was a little wild and full of enthusiasm. I made jam every chance I could; I badgered experienced farm ladies to teach me their tricks, I experimented with recipes I found in cookbooks and online, and then I developed my own recipes. I started Anarchy in a Jar in 2009 with a friend in the kitchen of my Brooklyn apartment. I had no business experience and I wasn't a trained chef or even a jam expert. All I had was energy, drive, curiosity, and a bunch of nice friends to help me. My first sales were at tasting parties I held in my apartment, and with those successes, I moved on to a small food market that had just begun in the basement of a church in Brooklyn. Within a few months, my jam was being sold at Whole Foods Market, I had appeared on *The Martha Stewart Show*, and I was featured in *T Magazine*, the *New York Times* style magazine.

I was lucky. Something was in the air all over New York City, and it swept me up and gave me and my fledgling company some wings. Small food businesses were spontaneously commencing around New York in the summer and fall of 2009, and many of us got our start in that church basement. Soon celebrities and famous food writers were visiting, and the press swarmed with joy at the newfound niche: a food-production renaissance blossoming in Brooklyn!

On a quiet backstreet in Greenpoint, Brooklyn, you can usually find me cooking jam in my small industrial kitchen. As customers and friends breeze in and out of the beer and cheese shop in the front of my kitchen, I fill jar after jar with jam that infuses the shop and the streets outside with the delicious aroma of stewed fruit. Condensing fruit and sugar into their precious essence, I spend most mornings bent over steaming pots, making my unique and tasty jam, jelly, preserves, marmalade, chutney, and pickled fruit. How did an Antarctic science worker transform into such a jam queen?

Jam making is in my blood. My father is an expert home cook and my mother is an avid canner. Growing up in upstate New York, I'd tag along with my mom as she gathered fruits and herbs, then I'd hang out in the kitchen and help as she preserved summer's bounty. In college, I became curious about food and food politics. The more I studied, the more I craved to cook and experiment with ingredients and flavors. The first batch of jam I made on my own was a disaster—there were strawberry stains all over my kitchen and the jam was the consistency of syrup. But I didn't give up. There was something there in the steady process and transformation of fresh fruit to preserved jam, and I was hooked.

When I was twenty-two, I spent a summer in western Massachusetts with friends and started making jam in earnest. I began to study flavor combinations and understand how different fruits needed varying levels of sugar and pectin. One of my friends was a nanny, and we would take the kids berry picking and jam in their beautiful kitchen in the afternoons as the kids napped. It was during that summer, on a warm night in August, high off the success of another jam session and excited by all life had to offer, that I thought, "This stuff is so pure, so good, and so intensely flavored . . . it's revolutionary . . . it's anarchy in a jar!"

Later, in my midtwenties, while traveling around the world in the off-months of my career with the United States Antarctic Program, I became more deeply interested in cooking and ingredients. Exploring the markets of Florence, Paris, and India, I found jams and preserves that blew my mind. Preserved Lemons? Pinot Noir Jelly? Apricot Rosemary Jam? I suddenly saw jam as a whole new creative canvas. Intrigued, I couldn't wait to get home and start experimenting.

When I returned to New York, I started making jam with a renewed focus, teaching friends how to make it and selling my creations at events and parties. Why did I make my own jam? I loved the process of condensing the essence of fruit into a pure and durable staple. I loved the chemical transformation that happens when you turn fresh fruit into a lasting substance. Most of all, I loved sharing what I made with others and seeing my passion and excitement passed along.

In 2005, there weren't many interesting jams being widely sold in stores here in the States. I occasionally came across great-tasting jams at farm stands or markets in California, but they were usually very simple and supersweet. They were not the kinds of jams I craved, the kinds I made myself that I could eat every day and put on toast or have with cheese and meat, using it as a versatile condiment.

Anarchy in a Jar was born organically in 2009 and continues to grow organically. Instead of the most common way a product is developed—someone thinks of a good product idea, then hires a co-packing factory to produce it, a marketing firm to advertise it, and minions to hawk it at trade shows and through advertising campaigns—my company started out from the ground up. We achieved every success through personal connections, networks, friends, and neighbors.

Within two months I was selling my jam at stores throughout Brooklyn, and within eight months the jam was on the shelves of Whole Foods Market and being described by Julia Moskin as "extraordinary" in the *New York Times*. The energy that comes from grassroots growth is addictive and viral, and it is part of the reason the jam classes I teach have been such a great success.

One of the unique things about my jam is the process, including where my fruit comes from. I have relationships with small farms, many of which are local. When buying fruit such as grapefruits, which don't grow nearby, I try to purchase it collaboratively with other purveyors and restaurants, like Print in Manhattan, so the fruit is driven directly from the farm to our kitchens.

My jam is often cooked for a short amount of time, sometimes with the addition of low-methoxyl pectin, which doesn't need sugar to gel, meaning that throughout the process I'm able to preserve the healthy properties of the fruit and the jam still tastes fresh. I believe enjoying jam and preserved fruits should be a pure pleasure, not a guilty one. By using a small amount or no sugar, I make jams that are healthier and with an improved flavor. Many recipes in this cookbook do not require sugar, although in most of the recipes some is recommended for flavor, color, and preservation. Jam is the condensed essence of fruit, and with the right balance of sugar and flavors, it becomes a precious and adroit staple. At almost every market, customers are surprised and delighted to find that my jam tastes like real fruit, and they often admit to eating it with a spoon straight out of the jar.

With less sugar and when created with unique flavors, the jams can be used in endless ways: in sandwiches with cheese and meat as well as traditionally with toast, yogurt, and desserts. Fans of our jam have come up with some delicious and creative combinations: Rhubarb and Hibiscus Jam as a glaze on pork ribs, Spiced Beer Jelly with a homemade mayo as a condiment for burgers, Hot Fireman's Pear Jam grilled with sharp Cheddar on rustic crusty bread, and more.

With this cookbook, I hope to share the knowledge I've gathered as well as delicious recipes you can enjoy at home and creative pairings that have been given to me by customers, jam students, and friends. To those who know me best, I'll always be the "jam lady," living and jamming according to my own personal dogma of making pure, delicious, handmade jam. I've learned that there's nothing freer or more human than taking control of your food, understanding where it's from and how it's made. It's a beautiful and simple thing to be able to preserve summer in a jar to share with family, friends, and neighbors.

It's a beautiful thing to be able to preserve summer in a jar.

THE BASICS

"No, jam cannot kill you" is often the way I begin my jam-making classes. There's a fear surrounding canning: you'll miss one step or one key ingredient, and the resulting jam will be poisonous. Although botulism and other harmful bacteria do exist, canning can be thoroughly safe if you are organized, learn the basics of preservation as described in this chapter, and follow the simple steps I outline later in "Get Your Jam On: The Step-by-Step Guide" (pages 23–31).

In this chapter, I'll answer the basic questions I get asked during my jam classes and workshops, such as "What's pectin and do I need it?" and "What's botulism, anyway?"

I'll start with ingredients and equipment. For many cooks and would-be canners, knowing where and how to acquire the right materials can be intimidating. Turn to "Sources" (page 250) to find stores, websites, and other nationwide resources where you can buy jars, pectin, and various canning equipment. There's no need to break the bank and buy tons of gadgets; most of the equipment I recommend you probably already have in your kitchen.

INGREDIENTS AND EQUIPMENT

Whether you are making jam, jelly, marmalade, pickled fruit, or syrups, preserving fruit requires attention to detail—from the type of fruit to the pot you use. This section provides a quick overview of what you need to start canning fruit at home.

Ingredients

Fruit Choose fresh, beautiful fruit. Frozen fruit (without syrup or sugar) will work, too, if you're jamming out of season. Fruit is the core of most jam recipes, so it's important to get the best you can find. Fresh, recently picked fruit is ideal. There's a myth that you should make jam with old, inedible fruit that's bruised or rotten, but if you use this kind of fruit, your jam will then taste like rotten or bruised fruit—gross! You can use imperfect fruit, but make sure to cut off the bad parts. Choose fruit that's ripe but not overripe, the kind of fruit you want to eat. Each fruit is unique and has properties that require a particular method of preservation to enhance its flavor and texture. Some recipes in this book require added pectin when the fruit does not have a significant quantity to gel naturally, allowing for a shorter cooking time and less added sugar, such as Wild Blueberry Jam (page 60). Some recipes use the peel and skin of the fruit and do not need added pectin to congeal, such as Purist Kumquat Marmalade (page 104) or Apricot Jam (page 48). Some recipes, especially those for preserves and marmalades, require macerating the fruit overnight to slowly soften it and to release the natural juices, such as Figalicious Jam (page 68).

Pectin (from the Greek πηκτικός; *pektikos*, "congealed, curdled") It's a structural heteropolysaccharide (try saying that three times fast!) that's in the primary cell walls of terrestrial plants and certain fruits. Pectin is produced commercially as off-white to light brown powder, mainly extracted from citrus fruits or apples, and is used in food as a gelling agent (particularly in jams and jellies). It's also used in many other edible products, such as medicines, stabilizers, and milk (as a source of fiber). Why use pectin? Sometimes people turn their noses up when I say I use pectin. They say things like, "My grandma never used pectin." First of all, old-school methods are not always better or healthier, and cooking lore is full of mythology that is not always accurate. Pectin is your friend, and it is part of any jam-making process, whether you choose to include the seeds and rind from citrus, make your own "pectin" jelly

When choosing ingredients, fresh, recently picked fruit is ideal.

from apples, or use a store-bought brand. Fruit has different levels of natural pectin depending on the variety (see the Natural Fruit Pectin Levels chart on page 12). The pectin you buy in the store is usually natural apple or citrus powder in a concentrated form. If you're making jam, then you're using pectin in one form or another. I recommend using low-methoxyl pectin, sold in the United States as Pomona's Universal Pectin. It's made of 100 percent citrus that has been processed into a fine powder. When this type of pectin is used with a small amount of calcium phosphate as an activator, the jam sets in a smooth and consistent gel without the need for sugar. Using low-methoxyl

pectin is the easiest way to create a nicely textured, low-sugar, high-quality jam that is less labor intensive than if you made your own pectin with apple jelly or citrus parts or through the use of excess sugar. Using this pectin also greatly reduces your cooking time, so the natural properties and flavor of the fruit are maintained. Basically, it enables you to make jam that tastes like fresh fruit.

An added bonus when using Pomona's Universal Pectin is that sugar is not required to make the jam congeal, so you can use other sweeteners, such as honey, maple syrup, agave, or stevia (see the "Sugar-Free" chapter on page 131).

See "Sources" on page 250 for information on where to purchase pectin.

Sugar Dry, granulated sugar is a key ingredient in most jam, jelly, preserves, and marmalades (see the "Sugar-Free" chapter on page 131 for alternatives). Sugar enhances the flavor, helps the gel to set correctly, preserves the color, increases the jam's shelf life once it's opened, and gives the product its satiny texture and glossy sheen. The recipes in this book call for the minimal amount of sugar for preservation; they're healthier and will allow the natural flavor of the fruit to be dominant. I believe canned fruit should still taste like fruit, and using only a little sugar will produce this effect. Using this lesser amount of sugar creates a versatile condiment that can be eaten with yogurt, on toast, and in a variety of dishes (see the "Pairings" chapter on page 199).

Lemon Juice Acid enhances and brightens fruit flavors as well as helps to create the right texture and set. Usually about two to three tablespoons per batch is necessary, but feel free to experiment with adding more or less. There are a few recipes in this book that require you to use more to ensure proper acidity for canning. If you prefer less or no lemon juice, you can purchase pH strips and test for pH. For proper preserving, your jam needs a pH that is around 3 to 4.6, but never higher.

Equipment
Candy Thermometer Most recipes in this book don't require a thermometer, but for some recipes I recommend using one to determine if the jam has reached 221°F, which is the temperature at which most jam will begin to gel. Once you get used to what jam looks like when it reaches this stage, you may not need the thermometer at all.

Choose fresh, beautiful fruit.

Jars and Lids The best brands are Ball and Kerr, who make Mason jars with two-piece lids that are designed for home canning. The jars are very strong and made to withstand processing in a hot water bath. Lids for canning are made for use with high-acid foods. The jars and metal rings can be reused, but the flat piece with the rubber flange should be used only once, as the rubber may not form a proper seal if reused. You can purchase the flat metal lids separately and reuse the other pieces.

Canning supplies are sometimes hard to find in urban areas. See "Sources" (page 250) for a list of places to purchase jars in New York City and online. Try hardware stores, such as Ace and True Value, and you can buy them from the hardware stores' websites, too. If you don't see the kind you would like at your local hardware store, ask them. Most stores will special order a case or more for you. Jars and lids are also available at some urban and suburban grocery stores, such as Kroger and Safeway. In New York City, you can find canning jars at cooking stores like Broadway Panhandler, the Brooklyn Kitchen, and Fishs Eddy. At hardware stores, eight-ounce jars are approximately $8 per dozen, including the lids and rings, while at specialty stores they can be as much as $18 per dozen. Lids often come with the jars in the same case. If you're purchasing them online, make sure they are thin, flat, round metal lids with a rubber gum flange or binder that seals them against the top of the jar and that they include a button in the center that pops down when sealed. It's important to have lids that seal with a proper rubber flange. This is the only type of lid that the FDA recommends. A button in the center of the lid that pops up when the jar is unsealed and stays down when the jar is properly sealed is the only way you will know if your jar has the proper vacuum seal. Many online stores

NATURAL FRUIT PECTIN LEVELS

High-Pectin Fruit	Medium-Pectin Fruit	Low-Pectin Fruit
crab apples, black currants, gooseberries, plums, red currants, cooking apples, cranberries, damson plums, quince, oranges, lemons, and most other citrus fruits (citrus peel and seeds are superhigh in pectin)	sour cherries, raspberries, loganberries, boysenberries, apricots, and tayberries	strawberries, blueberries, blackberries, rhubarb, elderberries, peaches, sweet cherries, sweet apples, pears, and figs

may sell you improper lids and/or jars if you do not specify—make sure they're food safe, heat safe, and can be processed in a water bath canner. See more information in the "Sources" chapter (page 250).

Make sure your jars are food safe, heat safe, and can be processed in a water bath canner.

Jar Funnel and Lifter A funnel and a jar lifter are very useful for filling and lifting jars. These aren't necessary, but they make the canning process much easier and less messy. You can substitute metal heat-safe tongs for the jar grabber if you're using jars that are eight ounces or smaller. Or you can purchase heat-proof and waterproof gloves and lift the jars out by hand, but make sure you get ones that will protect you from 212°F boiling water. You can buy funnels and lifters at many hardware or kitchen supply stores. They're cheap and should cost only a few dollars each. You can order them online, too. I find if you're using four-ounce or smaller jars, it's easier to use metal tongs than official jar lifters, because the lids are too small for proper gripping.

Large Pot for Processing A large nine-quart stockpot is required for processing your jars. Make sure it's deep enough to fit the jars *plus* two inches of water over the top of them.

Scale Most of the recipes in this book list the fruit by weight and by volume. Weighing your ingredients will be more accurate, but if you don't have a scale, weigh your ingredients when purchasing them at the grocery store or farmers' market and parcel out your fruit then and there.

Spoons and Ladles These are essential to have if you don't already own some. Use wood, stainless steel, or copper. For removing air bubbles from the jam, you can also use an old chopstick or a thin spatula.

A funnel can be very useful for filling jars.

Wide 6- to 8-Quart Preserving Pan or Pot You'll need this pot for cooking the jams. It should be wider than it is tall so that the liquid can evaporate more quickly during cooking. If you have only a deep, narrow pot, it will work but the cooking times might be inaccurate, because you would need to cook the jam for a longer time.

The pot should be at least 6 to 8 quarts in order to hold the ingredients and to prevent them from boiling over. Fill the pan only a third to half of the way up to prevent jams from boiling over.

Make sure the pan you use is nonreactive because fruit is high in corrosive acid. I recommend using a heavy-bottomed stainless-steel or enameled cast-iron one (such as Le Creuset or Staub), or a preserving pan (I love Mauviel copper preserving pans). Do not use aluminum, as it will negatively react with the acid in the fruit. If you use a thin pan, beware of scorching and uneven cooking. If you must use one, be vigilant and stir frequently.

Tools of the Trade

Food Mill This device separates fruit pulp, seeds, and skin from the juice; this tool is recommended for a number of recipes in this book.

Measuring Cups and Spoons Liquid measuring cups are handy. They're made to hold liquid and feature pouring spouts to prevent spilling. Dry measuring cups are effective for accurately leveling dry ingredients.

Metal Sheet Trays These can be used to roast or dry fruit, herbs, and spices.

Sieve and Cheesecloth or Jelly Bag A fine-mesh *chinois* sieve and multilayers of cheesecloth or a jelly bag are needed for straining fruit pulp from its juice for jellies, syrups, and shrubs.

Small Pots and Pans These are useful for making syrups and blanching ingredients.

Zester A long thin microplane with a half-inch metal row of sharp holes does a great job of producing fine, thin strips of peel.

GETTING ORGANIZED AND GETTING STARTED

To become a canner, you need curiosity, ingredients, a kitchen (even if it's small), a few tools, and an idea of what you want to preserve. But where do you start? Curiosity is a good place to begin, along with an open mind that takes pleasure in the process and the execution. Many cooks enjoy thinking creatively about food and imagining how flavor combinations might taste. But ideas come with experience, and you have to practice a few canning recipes before you start coming up with your own creations.

I like to let the fruit lead me—I pick what's fresh and in season, and then I dream up interesting flavor mixtures to play with. Once I have a recipe in mind, I start planning my approach and procuring the ingredients. Once prepared, you can focus more on the process and have fun. When you are first learning to preserve, follow these basic rules to get you off and jamming:

Dream Start by choosing a fruit. Every recipe has a particular fruit at its core. After you decide what fruit you'd like to work with and find a recipe, figure out how you can get the best-quality fruit you can find. Are there other ingredients? Once you have a plan on how to procure your ingredients, you're almost there.

Plot Strategize your jam session. Do you have the jars? The pot? A cheesecloth? A thermometer? If you need to, lay out your materials so you can plot out your plan. I like to make lists and drawings to visualize my strategy on paper so I can determine if I'm prepared to start jamming.

Record As you begin experimenting with canning fruit, take notes on the process and note each variation you choose. This is the key to success, as this record will allow you to retrace your steps and improve each batch.

THE ART AND CRAFT OF CANNING AT HOME

Art is the expression or application, both in product and process, of human creative skill and imagination. It often takes a visual or auditory form, such as painting, sculpture, or music; but at its core, most art is rendered through making something beautiful or evocative. I know when I'm under the spell of creativity because I enter a kind of trance, and during that trance something special happens that can't quite be defined. Craft is a little different; craft is usually defined as an activity involving skill, studied knowledge, and learned practice in making things by hand. Craft traditionally involves a systematic approach to mastering a level of knowledge, which requires a certain amount of education and practice.

Preserving fruit requires a delicate combination of both art and craft. It requires skill, basic knowledge of canning science, and repeated practice to perfect the product. In preserving, you need craft to make jam that is edible and safe. Once you know the basics and hone your skills, you can advance in the art of preservation and make something that's special and uniquely yours.

Understanding Fruit Preservation

Knowing how the process of preserving fruit works allows you to be confident as you begin canning and to be assured that your friends or family will be safe to enjoy your homemade goods.

Microorganisms Planet Earth is teaming with microorganisms, molds, and yeasts. Our food and water contain them, and they occur naturally as the building blocks of life: birth, growth, and decay. Humans are basically bags of water filled with proteins and bacteria, with the number of bacteria in our bodies outnumbering cells by almost 10 to 1! But when preparing food environments for preservation, you need to understand how to control bacteria in order to prevent spoilage and contamination.

Microorganisms that cause food to spoil need specific conditions to survive: they need water, temperatures between 40°F and 139°F, oxygen, and low acid. Most fruit has a natural water content, and canned foods are meant to be stored at room temperature, so that means for canning, we need to focus on the last two conditions to create safe products: limit air contamination and ensure high acidity.

Preservation A to Z Processing the filled jars in a hot water bath to seal them creates an anaerobic environment, an airless vacuum, where microorganisms cannot survive. How does that work? When the jars are placed in a boiling water bath, the jars and the food inside heat up. As the food heats up, it expands, forcing air out of the lids, which have yet to seal as they jiggle around in the boiling water. When you remove the jars from the pot of hot water, they start to cool, and as they cool, the food contracts, the lid presses tightly to the rim of the jar, and a vacuum seal is created. You can hear the sound of the button in the center of the lid make a popping noise as it is sucked down. It's a very satisfying sound that lets you know you were successful in the final stage of canning. Creating an airtight vacuum seal both prevents microorganisms from entering and also creates an airless environment inside the jar where they can't live, in case any snuck in while you were filling the jars.

The last condition that must be met in order to safely preserve fruit is to create a highly acidic environment. All the recipes in this book are for high-acid foods that have a pH below 4.6; this level of acid is sufficient to prevent the growth of microorganisms and make sure their spores cannot be activated. Most fruits are naturally acidic—with the exception of figs and tomatoes, which can sometimes have insufficient acidity (recipes for these include specific canning instructions). Preserves made with most fruit, such as jams, jellies, marmalades, and chutneys, will naturally have enough levels of acid. Vegetables are low in acid, but if you add acid, such as in the form of vinegar, they can be safely processed in a water bath.

Vegetables and fruit can be pickled either by adding acid through vinegar or lemon juice, or they can be fermented to the point where beneficial bacteria has converted the natural sugars into lactic acid, thus lowering the pH to a safe level, below 4.6. Foods that ferment in salt (such as Moroccan Preserved Lemons on page 176) are preserved by the acid that's created but also by the salt (bad bacteria don't like salt or acid), so using the recommended quantity of salt is important to prevent spoilage.

To summarize, you need to remember to heat the jam to kill off microorganisms, process the filled jars to create a vacuum seal and prevent growth, and use high-acid foods or add acid in order to create an environment that's uninviting for microorganisms. Voilà!

The Revolution Starts in Your Mouth

Great artists have an intrinsic understanding of their materials. As a stone sculptor, you need to understand how marble will feel, move, and interact with the elements. As a fruit preserver, you need to know how your ingredients will interact with one another in the jar and in the mouth.

Taste and Flavor There are five basic tastes in the world: sweet, sour, bitter, salty, and umami. Ideally, you should harness all five and balance them in perfect harmony. As you create flavors, think about how each component will feel in the mouth as someone eats it. For Hot Fireman's Pear Jam (page 65), the flavors of chipotle and cinnamon emerge after the taste of sweetness; the spiciness is a slow-building heat that warms in the mouth after a few moments. This is a very different type of mouth experience than what you have when you sample I Eat NYC Hot Pepper Jelly (page 79), which has an immediate heat from the vinegar and hot peppers, and which tempers well with cheese.

Texture and Consistency Seeds and peel will greatly affect the texture of your canned fruit. Texture is personal, and everyone has his or her own inclinations. Some people hate or love seeds, some people hate or love slivers of peel. To make a great product, you need to understand how texture will affect the feeling and taste. When making marmalade, you may want to slice the peels very finely or leave them longer; when making a berry jam, you may wish to process the jam through a food mill to remove the seeds or to work with the slightly bitter but more flavorful taste of keeping them in. The amount of pectin and the length of cooking time will also greatly affect the consistency of each preserved product. As you gain experience, experiment with these components to create your ideal consistency. I strive for velvety and smooth, with just enough gel so that the jam is spreadable but loose enough so that it slides and melts along the tongue.

Becoming a Jamarchist

As you perfect the craft of preserving fruit and begin to understand your materials, you can start becoming an artist—a jamarchist.

Experiment with flavor combinations. Each chapter includes a Make It Your Own section at the end, with suggestions for alternative herb, spice, and alcohol combinations. Begin by adding small amounts and keep notes so you can adjust the ratios with each new batch. Adding or subtracting liquids, in particular, may require you to add more or less pectin. Experiment with flavor combinations and go wild—there are no boundaries as long as you adhere to the ratios of ingredients and a proper pH level. Start a revolution in your kitchen. Here are some tips to keep in mind as you try new inventions:

Sugar Granulated cane sugar is used for the sugar in most of these recipes, but you can experiment with turbinado, brown, or raw organic sugar. Unrefined sugars make jams with a particular flavor and may require longer cooking or an

alternative pectin distribution, so be vigilant in your documentation and don't get discouraged if your initial product tastes weird or has an odd texture.

Use classic flavor combinations as your inspiration when adding herbs and spices.

Booze Alcohol will increase the liquid content of each recipe, so adjust the pectin and sugar content accordingly when adding alcohol. It will also affect the flavor and may taste stronger than you predict, so start with one or two ounces per recipe and cautiously increase the ratio for taste.

Herbs and Spices Almost all the recipes in this book use herbs and spices to enhance the flavors of the core fruit ingredient. I definitely recommend substituting and adding new ones. Use classic flavor combinations as your inspiration. Cocktails, desserts, and sauces all use fruit along with herbs and spices to create unique flavors and are good muses for your preservation experimentation.

Take a deep breath, because now you're ready to start canning some fruit. Jam on!

GET YOUR JAM ON:
THE STEP-BY-STEP GUIDE

After teaching numerous classes over the years, I've come to realize that people want more in-depth instruction than most recipes tend to offer so they can truly understand what they're making. So in order for you to understand the basic process of canning fruit before you jump in, here's an overview of the steps you'll take to make many of the jam and jelly recipes in this book.

I have deconstructed a recipe for a berry jam, such as 3's Company Triple-Berry Jam or Strawberry Balsamic Jam, but the steps are very similar for many of the jam and jelly recipes in this book. Also, steps 10 through 12 can be applied to all the recipes that require a water bath technique. The recipe described on the following pages uses added low-methoxyl citrus pectin. Not all recipes in this book require added pectin, but many of the recipes in the "Jam and Jelly" chapter use it to make a quick-cooked, fresh-flavored product.

As you'll see, the process is really pretty simple. Once you know the basics, you can get playful and creative by adding ingredients, textures, and flavors. But let's start from the beginning.

STEP 1: **GET THE FRUIT**

Fresh, recently picked fruit is ideal. Farmers' markets, pick-your-own farms, fruit stands, or your local CSA (Community Supported Agriculture) are the best places to find good fruit, as their produce is usually picked recently. Picking your own fruit is of course the most fun, but not always possible for everyone. Many grocery stores also carry fresh local fruit. For berries, if you can't get fresh fruit, frozen fruit (without added sugar or syrup) is a good substitute—use it over out-of-season berries that have been shipped from far away. Out-of-season fruit is usually picked unripe and allowed to ripen on the shelf, which results in bland flavor and less developed sugar content. Frozen fruit has been picked ripe and frozen immediately, and its flavors have been

Taken at Brooklyn Grange rooftop farm

preserved at their peak, and small farms often freeze their crops so that they can continue to sell them throughout the year. Before using frozen fruit in a recipe throw them in the fridge for a day to defrost, then follow the instructions in each recipe the same way as you would with fresh fruit.

For fresh fruit, make sure it's rinsed with any hulls or stems removed.

See "Sources" (page 250) and "Laena's Favorite Fruit Farms" (page 256) for information about farms that offer pick-your-own produce and a list of sources for finding fruit in New York and elsewhere in the United States.

STEP 2: WASH AND SANITIZE JARS AND LIDS

Jars The first thing you'll want to do is get your jars ready. If you have a dishwasher with a sanitize cycle, use it to thoroughly sanitize the jars quickly. Leave the jars in the dishwasher on "heated dry" until you are ready to use them. If you don't have a dishwasher, you can wash the jars in hot, soapy water and rinse them, then place them in a large pot of water. Make sure they're covered by an inch of water above the top of the jars; stacking them in the pot is fine. Bring the water to a boil, then turn off the heat and let them sit in the hot water until you are ready to use them. Boiling them longer is unnecessary; heat processing them in a water bath—as you'll do after you make the jam and fill the jars—will destroy any microorganisms in the food and in the containers and lids. It's important to keep the jars hot so they don't shatter when you fill them with hot jam.

After sanitizing, it's important to keep the jars hot so they don't shatter when you fill them with hot jam.

Lids If you are using two-part lids, leave the screw bands to the side, as they don't need to be heated. Put the lids (the flat part of two-piece lids) into a pot of hot but not quite boiling water—boiling them for any length of time can melt or disfigure the rubber. While you cook the fruit, let the lids rest in the hot water with the pot covered so that the rubber inside the lid stays warm—this will help the lids create a firm seal.

STEP 3: CRUSH THE FRUIT

Crushing the fruit is not necessary for all jams, so make sure you follow the specific instructions for the fruit and style you're making.

Depending on the recipe, I recommend using your hands or a potato masher to create a uniform texture and to release the juice of larger fruits, such as strawberries or pears. If you are using your hands, wear gloves, as many people are allergic to fruit acid on their skin. There's no need to be perfectly uniform in crushed fruit; most people prefer chunks of fruit in their jam. If you want a completely smooth jam, you can use a food processor or a blender.

If you want to make seedless jam, you will need to process the crushed berries through a food mill. I like seeds; they enhance the flavor by adding a hint of bitterness and texture.

You can crush the fruit with your hands, a potato masher, a food processor, or a blender, depending on the consistency you are hoping to achieve.

STEP 4: MEASURE OUT THE SUGAR AND PECTIN

Depending on which type of jam you're making, you may need to use a differing amount of fruit, sugar, and pectin. The precise measurements can be found in each recipe.

A number of the jam and jelly recipes in this cookbook call for low-methoxyl citrus pectin, which uses calcium phosphate to activate a powdered citrus pectin in order to make a jam gel. You'll want to use Pomona's Universal Pectin (to purchase, see "Sources" on page 250), which comes with two pouches: one has one teaspoon of calcium powder and the other has nine teaspoons citrus pectin. The pectin gets mixed into the sugar, and the calcium powder gets mixed with water. Mix ½ teaspoon of the calcium water with ½ cup water. You'll need only a few teaspoons of this calcium-water mixture for each recipe in this book, and it can be reused if refrigerated.

For many recipes, you'll calculate about half the amount of sugar as fruit, so if you're using 4 cups of fruit, you'll need 2 cups sugar. Mix the dry pectin with about 1 cup of the sugar. Mix thoroughly; I find a fork works great.

In preparation for testing the gel later on, keep a few metal spoons cool in a glass of ice water or in the freezer while you complete the next few steps.

STEP 5: COOK THE FRUIT

Measure the crushed berries and place them in a nonreactive stainless-steel, copper, or cast-iron pot or preserving pan. Add 3 teaspoons calcium water for every 4 cups of fruit, and stir to combine.

Lemon juice is a great addition to any jam, and the acid in it helps enhance the flavor and set the texture. It will also brighten the color and prevent the jam from turning brown. Add it now, usually 3 tablespoons for every 4 cups of fruit.

Bring the fruit to a boil over medium-high heat, stirring often to prevent scorching. Fruit has lots of natural sugar, so it burns easily.

Add herbs, liquor, or spices if you're using them, and stir to combine, being careful not to get burned by the hot jam (sometimes it spits).

Many jams foam while they cook, especially strawberry, peach, and pear jams. The foam is simply air produced from vigorous boiling. It's not poisonous or harmful, but I suggest you remove it for maximum taste, attractiveness, and texture.

I love saving the skimmed foam and using it in cocktails or on cereal or desserts. Pour a little in some soda water for an instant and delicious strawberry soda!

STEP 6: ADD PECTIN AND SUGAR MIXTURE

If the recipe calls for vinegar, add it now. When the jam is at a rolling and steady boil that cannot be stirred down, slowly stir in the pectin and sugar mixture, stirring vigorously all the while. Stir constantly; remember to stir around the bottom and sides, it will take 1 to 2 minutes to dissolve the pectin.

When the jam reaches a steady rolling boil, add the sugar and pectin mixture.

STEP 7: **ADD REMAINING SUGAR**

When the berry-pectin mixture has reached a full boil, add any sugar that remains and return to a boil. Skim off any and all foam that has formed at the top and let the jam boil for 1 minute. Remove from the heat. Do a final skim for foam if there's any left.

STEP 8: **TEST FOR GEL**

When the jam is done, use one of the cooled metal spoons to scoop up a small amount and let it cool to room temperature, about 30 seconds. If it thickens up to the consistency desired, then it's ready. I like to test the gel by pushing my index finger against the jam: If the jam wrinkles up, as if it's forming a skin, then I know it's ready. If it seems loose and too syrupy, mix in a little more pectin (start with ½ teaspoon) with at least ¼ cup sugar and bring the jam to a boil again for 1 minute.

My jam students often ask, "Why didn't it set?" Most jam needs pectin, sugar, and acid in order to thicken properly and be jamlike. Each fruit has a unique amount of natural pectin (see the chart in the pectin section of the "Basics" chapter on page 12), and some that have medium to low levels need pectin added (via powdered pectin, citrus skins or apple, or extra-long cooking time) to set right.

Making jam is about finding the right balance of pectin, sugar, and acidity. In addition, it takes at least one minute of vigorous boiling to provide enough heat to meld the three into harmony. So if your jam doesn't firm up, you need to improve the balance of these three and add more pectin, sugar, or acid (such as lemon juice), or boil it a little harder. Again, sugar scorches easily, so remember to stir the jam a few times during the final minute of boiling.

STEP 9: **LET IT REST**

If you let the jam rest for two minutes after turning off the heat, it will start to gel just a little. One final stir will help the jam be more consistent in texture and will prevent your fruit from floating to the top if there's a lot of juice.

If you don't want to preserve the jam or bother with the canning process, then stop here and put the jam in the fridge; it will last a few weeks.

Read on if you want to fill jars and process them in a water bath. If canned, your jam will keep for at least a year. Plus it's much more fun to give your creations as presents or unveil them at a dinner party a few months later when they're in canning jars.

If canned, your jams will keep for at least a year.

STEP 10: **FILL THE JARS**

Fill your jars to within a ¼ inch of the top for jam, jelly, marmalade, and preserves and to within a ½ inch for chutney, pickles, syrups, and shrubs.

If the mixture is thick and chunky (such as chutney), slide a chopstick or thin rubber spatula down between the food and inside of the jar two or three times to release any air bubbles. Air bubbles can cause seal failure or discoloration.

Wipe the rims of the jars with a clean damp paper towel or cloth, removing any food particles from the top and sides. Food left on the rim can prevent a proper vacuum seal from forming.

Place the flat metal lid on top and tighten with the separate ring; tighten the lid gently, not body-builder-tight, just hand-tight; place them into the pot full of boiling water (the same one you used to sanitize the jars). Tongs or jar lifters makes this much easier. Make sure all the jars are placed upright. It's fine to stack them on top of one another; just

make sure they are upright. You don't need a rack or any other gadgets; the jars are made to withstand heat and water-bath canning. Racks are fine if you would like to use them; they elevate the jars off the bottom, allowing for maximum heat circulation, and help keep the jars upright if you have a large pot and only a few jars.

STEP 11: PROCESS JARS

Keep the jars covered with at least two inches of water above the top of them and cover the pot with a tight-fitting lid.

Most recipes in this book require boiling for six to ten minutes (each recipe specifies the exact processing time). After they boil for the specified time, turn off the heat and let the jars rest in the hot water for two more minutes before you remove them from the pot to cool.

Some people are a little lazy and don't process the jars. If you fill the jars with super hot jam, put the lids on, and invert them, they will probably seal. But this is not a proper method for preservation and it won't kill the harmful bacterium that causes spoilage. Hot water bath canning heats food to 212°F (110°C), which is a temperature that's sufficient to kill mold, yeast, and most bacteria found in high-acid foods. If you're bothering to make jam, either put it in the fridge and eat it right away or process it in a water bath using the proper method described above. For more in-depth geeky information on the art and science of canning, see the "Basics" chapter on page 7.

STEP 12: REMOVE, COOL, RELAX

Use a jar-lifter tool or regular kitchen tongs to lift the jars out of the water. Be very careful—they're hot and slippery!

Let the jars set on the counter for at least six hours and preferably overnight to allow them to cool undisturbed. Once they're cool, you can then remove the rings and put pretty fabric over the top and add labels, if you prefer.

Check that the jars are sealed by pressing gently in the center of the lid with your finger. If it pops up and down, it's not sealed. If it's firm and doesn't move, then it's sealed. If it's not sealed, don't panic, just put the jar in the refrigerator and you can still use it—breakfast tomorrow!

Once the jars have cooled, store them in a dark place like a cupboard or closet; sunlight can fade the color. They will last approximately twelve months on the shelf. After six to eight months, they may darken in color and start to separate or become less gelled.

Jam will last approximately two to four months once opened and refrigerated. Often they'll last much longer; you know a jam has gone bad when mold forms on top.

Phew, you're done! Sit down, eat your delicious jam, and be superproud of yourself.

Be careful when removing your jars from the hot water.

4

JAM AND JELLY

Jam and jelly are the most common styles of preserving fruit. Jam is mashed fruit pulp cooked with sweetener to a smooth, congealed consistency. Jelly is the strained juice of fruit cooked to a translucent and congealed consistency. These are great Canning 101 recipes, as they tend to be the simplest to perfect and take the shortest amount of time to prepare. If you're new to jamming, the sweet and tart 3's Company Triple-Berry Jam is a good beginner jam, but you'll soon advance to the more complicated, warm, and spicy Hot Fireman's Pear Jam.

The recipes in this chapter are organized by seasonality and style, starting with the early-spring Rhubarb and Hibiscus Jam and Strawberry Balsamic Jam and ending with I Eat NYC Hot Pepper Jelly, which can be made in the late fall.

In Make It Your Own Jam and Jelly on pages 82–83, an extensive list of unique flavor combinations and ingredients is provided so that you may customize your own flavors.

Rhubarb and Hibiscus Jam

Strawberry Balsamic Jam

3's Company Triple-Berry Jam

Raspberry Rye Whiskey Jam

Apricot Jam

Sugar Plum Fairy Jam

Really Rosie Jam

Thai Me Up Jam

Wild Blueberry Jam

Hot Fireman's Pear Jam

Figalicious Jam

Watermelon and Lemongrass Jelly

Finger Lakes Wine Grape Jelly

Spiced Beer Jelly

I Eat NYC Hot Pepper Jelly

RHUBARB AND HIBISCUS JAM

| Tart rhubarb gets a color boost and a floral, fruity kick from hibiscus flowers |

One of the first things to arrive at the farmers' market in early spring is rhubarb. Right before the first strawberries, these earthy, tart, and sour weeds burst out of the still-cold earth to remind us that the seasons have cycled through once more and the glorious days of warmth and good produce are just beginning.

I sell this flavor at outdoor food markets in the spring and summer, and customers often remark that they've never heard of rhubarb before. Rhubarb is a stalk that grows like a weed in most parts of the country. The leaves are poisonous, but the stalks are delicious! It's a natural tart partner in strawberry pie and is often used to enliven early-spring dishes. I love rhubarb all on its own, without showy strawberries to steal its thunder. But the ugly brown color of rhubarb jam is not so appealing, so I like to add hibiscus flowers to color it magenta and boost its herbal and fruity flavor.

This jam appears slightly complicated because it takes two days from start to finish, but it's actually pretty simple. The first day's steps are preparation and can be done in ten minutes when you get back from the market or grocery store with your rhubarb. The next day, it will take you about an hour to cook the jam and process the jars.

Makes About Five 8-Ounce Jars or Two Pint Jars

INGREDIENTS

3 pounds rhubarb (about 9 cups diced)
3 tablespoons lemon juice
4 cups sugar (2 pounds)

For the Hibiscus Simple Syrup
½ cup water
1 cup sugar (½ pound)
1 tablespoon dried hibiscus flowers

PREP

For the rhubarb:

Rinse and dice the rhubarb; take care to use a sharp knife as the rhubarb is stringy and it takes a strong chop to separate. Measure the fruit into a glass bowl or a plastic food-safe Tupperware container and add the lemon juice and sugar.

FOR THE HIBISCUS SIMPLE SYRUP:

In a small saucepan, bring the water, sugar, and hibiscus flowers to a boil over medium-high; simmer until the sugar is dissolved and the color is bright magenta, about 3 minutes. Remove from the heat and let cool completely.

Add to the diced rhubarb mixture. Stir well. Do not refrigerate, but leave out on your counter overnight or up to 48 hours so that the sugar and lemon juice are allowed to help release the juice of the rhubarb. (It's pretty cool to watch the rhubarb release its juices!)

Once the juice is released, measure the fruit mixture into a 6- to 8-quart nonreactive pot; stir well.

FOR THE JARS AND LIDS:

Wash and rinse the jars; put them into a big stockpot; cover the jars with water and bring to a boil; turn off the heat. Let stand in hot water until you are ready to fill.

Bring the lids and rings to a boil; turn off the heat. Let stand in hot water until you are ready to screw them onto the jars.

Place a few metal spoons in the freezer for testing the consistency and gel of your jam later. You can also place them in a cup of ice water, if you prefer.

COOK

Bring the fruit to a boil over high heat, stirring frequently so it doesn't scorch. Gradually reduce the heat if the jam starts to stick and scorch; continue to cook for about 20 more minutes, until the jam is no longer watery and seems nicely thickened. Keep a watchful eye and stir vigilantly for the last 5 to 10 minutes to keep it from scorching. When the jam seems thickened and gelled, reduce the heat to low and test for consistency.

Pectin gels completely when thoroughly cool, so don't worry if your jam looks loose while still hot. To test, place a teaspoon of the hot jam onto one of the prepped frozen spoons. Place it back in the freezer, with the jam on it, for 3 to 4 minutes. Remove the spoon and test the gel by tilting the spoon vertically. What's the consistency? If the jam runs loosely like syrup then it's not done yet, but if it glides slowly along in a gloopy glob, then the jam is ready. If it is syrupy, bring it to a boil again for 1 to 5 minutes. This jam recipe has a naturally looser consistency than some of the other jams in this book, but it should still be spreadable.

Once done, give it a quick stir and turn off the heat.

PRESERVE

See pages 29–30 for in-depth instructions on filling and processing the jars.

For this recipe, process the jars in a boiling water bath for 6 minutes.

TIPS

Pairs well with strong, punchy blue cheese, such as Stilton, Gorgonzola, and Valdeón; great on crostini with prosciutto and radish; one customer suggests using it as a glaze on pork ribs; delicious on top of thick Greek yogurt. See Make It Your Own on pages 82–83 for unique flavor combinations and ingredients you can use to customize your own flavor.

STRAWBERRY BALSAMIC JAM

| Strawberries get a drizzle of balsamic vinegar to enhance their sweetness |

In this recipe, balsamic vinegar adds a rich acid that enhances the flavor of the fruit and makes it pop with strawberry intenseness. It also adds depth and a nice tang. You can use any type of balsamic vinegar, but the more aged, the better. You can increase the ratio with a tablespoon or two more if you fancy a more savory and vinegary jam. Small and supersweet, fresh strawberries are one of the best things about early summertime, and they are the best type to use for this recipe. Look for varieties such as Mara des Bois or Earliglow. You can often find quite flavorful strawberries at farmers' markets in cities and towns throughout the United States and Europe from May until August (see "Sources" on page 250). If you can't find the small variety, you can use any fresh strawberries for this recipe. If you're jamming in the winter, I suggest using frozen berries instead of the bland ones you will find fresh at the grocery store—grocery store berries are less flavorful, plus they have a lot of white inner flesh that will make your jam an unattractive brown color.

Makes About Four 8-Ounce Jars or Two Pint Jars

INGREDIENTS

3½ pounds strawberries (about 8 cups diced)
3 tablespoons lemon juice
3 cups sugar (1½ pounds)
3 tablespoons aged balsamic vinegar

For the Gelling

See Chapter 3 for more information on pectin and calcium water
5 teaspoons calcium water
4 teaspoons pectin

PREP

For the strawberries:

Rinse the berries and remove their hulls (green stems and leaves), then roughly dice. Measure the fruit into a 6- to 8-quart nonreactive pot and add lemon juice and the proper amount of calcium water into the pan; stir well.

FOR THE JARS AND LIDS:

Wash and rinse the jars; put them into a big stockpot; cover the jars with water and bring to a boil; turn off the heat. Let stand in hot water until you are ready to fill.

Bring the lids and rings to a boil; turn off the heat. Let stand in hot water until you are ready to screw them onto the jars.

Place a few metal spoons in the freezer for testing the consistency and gel of your jam later. You can also place them in a cup of ice water, if you prefer.

FOR THE SUGAR AND PECTIN:

Measure the sugar into a separate bowl or measuring cup and thoroughly mix the proper amount of pectin powder into the sugar—using a fork helps to disperse the pectin into the sugar. Set the sugar mixture aside.

COOK

Bring the fruit to a boil over medium-high heat. If it starts to foam, skim the foam off the top and discard the foam. Add the balsamic vinegar and return to a boil.

Pour the pectin-sugar mixture into the boiling jam slowly and carefully, stirring as you add. Stir vigorously 1 to 2 minutes to dissolve the pectin.

Return the fruit to a boil and remove from the heat. Skim off any and all foam that has formed on the top.

Pectin gels completely when thoroughly cool, so don't worry if your jam looks loose while still hot. To test, place a teaspoon of the hot jam onto one of the prepped frozen spoons; let it cool to room temperature (about 30 seconds) on the spoon. If it thickens up to the consistency desired, then the jam is ready. If not, mix in a little more pectin (½ teaspoon into ¼ cup sugar) and bring it to a boil again for 1 minute.

PRESERVE

See pages 29–30 for in-depth instructions on filling and processing the jars.

For this recipe, process the jars in a boiling water bath for 6 minutes.

TIPS

Pairs well with fresh cheeses such as goat cheese like chèvre and fresh ricotta; also good with punchy blue cheeses such as Valdeón and Gorgonzola; great on a sandwich with steak and Stilton; delicious on top of ice cream or yogurt. See Make It Your Own on pages 82–83 for unique flavor combinations and ingredients you can use to customize your own flavor.

3's COMPANY TRIPLE-BERRY JAM

| With blackberries, raspberries, and blueberries—oh my!
It's simply delicious, triple-berry perfection |

This is a toast-perfect jam, with a great mix of sweet and tart flavors. It's perfect for those who love pure fruit flavor and an easy eating jam. Kids love this, too. I have a few young jam fans who visit my market booth every Sunday with their parents so they can buy a new jar.

This is a fast and simple jam to make, and a great one to start with if you're a novice or if you're making jam for picky eaters. If you prefer a more tart or sweet flavor, you may adjust the sugar ratio by a half cup less or more, respectively.

Makes About Eight 8-Ounce Jars or Two Pint Jars

INGREDIENTS

1 pound 2 ounces raspberries (about 3 cups)
1 pound 2 ounces blueberries (about 3¾ cups)
1 pound 2 ounces blackberries (about 3 cups)
3 tablespoons lemon juice
3 cups sugar (1½ pounds)

FOR THE GELLING
See Chapter 3 for more information on pectin and calcium water
3 teaspoons calcium water
2 teaspoons pectin

PREP

FOR THE BERRIES:
Rinse the berries and remove their stems. Measure the fruit into a 6- to 8-quart nonreactive pot and add the lemon juice and the proper amount of calcium water into the pan; stir well.

FOR THE JARS AND LIDS:
Wash and rinse the jars; put them into a big stockpot; cover the jars with water and bring to a boil; turn off the heat. Let stand in hot water until you are ready to fill.

Bring the lids and rings to a boil; turn off the heat. Let stand in hot water until you are ready to screw them onto the jars.

Place a few metal spoons in the freezer for testing the consistency and gel of your jam later. You can also place them in a cup of ice water, if you prefer.

For the sugar and pectin:

Measure the sugar into a separate bowl or measuring cup and thoroughly mix the proper amount of pectin powder into the sugar—using a fork helps to disperse the pectin into the sugar. Set the sugar mixture aside.

COOK

Bring the fruit to a boil over medium-high heat. If it starts to foam, skim the foam off the top and discard the foam.

Pour the pectin-sugar mixture into the boiling jam slowly and carefully, stirring as you add. Stir vigorously 1 to 2 minutes to dissolve the pectin.

Return the fruit to a boil and remove from the heat. Skim off any and all foam that has formed on the top.

Pectin gels completely when thoroughly cool, so don't worry if your jam looks loose while still hot. To test, place a teaspoon of the hot jam onto one of the prepped frozen spoons; let it cool to room temperature (about 30 seconds) on the spoon. If it thickens up to the consistency desired, then the jam is ready. If not, mix in a little more pectin (½ teaspoon into ¼ cup sugar) and bring it to a boil again for 1 minute.

PRESERVE

See pages 29–30 for in-depth instructions on filling and processing the jars.

For this recipe, process the jars in a boiling water bath for 6 minutes.

TIPS

Pairs well with fresh cheese like ricotta; great on ginger scones with clotted cream (recipe on page 205), or spooned into a cup of tea like the British do; delicious on top of ice cream or yogurt. See Make It Your Own on pages 82–83 for unique flavor combinations and ingredients you can use to customize your own flavor.

RASPBERRY RYE WHISKEY JAM

| *Tart raspberries get an exhilarating twist with rye whiskey and mint* |

Raspberry is secretly one of my favorite jam flavors. Plain raspberry jam is just fine, but with a little rye whiskey and some fresh mint, it becomes phenomenal.

Raspberries grow amazingly well in the Northwest, imbued with a deeply tart and intense flavor. Of course, you can find great raspberries throughout the United States in July and August. But if you can't get good fresh ones, frozen is also fine. I really like organic frozen raspberries from Oregon, which you can find in many gourmet bodegas or grocery stores.

Adding a little rye whiskey intensifies and enriches the flavor of the berries. Whereas bourbon is sweet and scotch is smoky, rye is spicy and adds a distinct flavor to the raspberries that heightens their tartness and adds a warm finish to the jam. Thanks to those avid drinkers who appreciate reviving old-fashioned cocktails, rye has become trendy again over the past few years. Before Prohibition, it was one of the most popular alcohols in the United States, and George Washington is rumored to have distilled his own secret batches. Adding a pinch of fresh spearmint is a wonderful enhancement to the berries. Try other kinds of mint, too, like lemon mint or—my favorite—chocolate mint!

This is an easy and quick jam to make, and a great jam to start with if you're new to canning.

Makes About Six 8-Ounce Jars or Two Pint Jars

INGREDIENTS
2 pounds fresh raspberries (about 4 cups)
2 tablespoons lemon juice
1½ cups sugar (¾ pound)
2 ounces rye whiskey
2 tablespoons fresh mint, minced finely

FOR THE GELLING
See Chapter 3 for more information on pectin and calcium water
5 teaspoons calcium water
4 teaspoons pectin

PREP

FOR THE RASPBERRIES:

Rinse and measure the berries into a 6- to 8-quart nonreactive pot and add the lemon juice and the proper amount of calcium water into the pan; stir well.

FOR THE JARS AND LIDS:

Wash and rinse the jars; put them into a big stockpot; cover the jars with water and bring to a boil; turn off the heat. Let stand in hot water until you are ready to fill.

Bring the lids and rings to a boil; turn off the heat. Let stand in hot water until you are ready to screw them onto the jars.

Place a few metal spoons in the freezer for testing the consistency and gel of your jam later. You can also place them in a cup of ice water, if you prefer.

FOR THE SUGAR AND PECTIN:

Measure the sugar into a separate bowl or measuring cup and thoroughly mix the proper amount of pectin powder into the sugar—using a fork helps to disperse the pectin into the sugar. Set the sugar mixture aside.

COOK

Bring the fruit to a boil over medium-high heat. If it starts to foam, skim the foam off the top and discard the foam. Add the rye whiskey and mint and stir to incorporate. Bring to a boil again.

Pour the pectin-sugar mixture into the boiling jam slowly and carefully, stirring as you add. Stir vigorously 1 to 2 minutes to dissolve the pectin.

Return the fruit to a boil and remove from the heat. Skim off any and all foam that has formed on the top.

Pectin gels completely when thoroughly cool, so don't worry if your jam looks loose while still hot. To test, place a teaspoon of the hot jam onto one of the prepped frozen spoons; let it cool to room temperature (about 30 seconds) on the spoon. If it thickens up to the consistency desired, then the jam is ready. If not, mix in a little more pectin (½ teaspoon into ¼ cup sugar) and bring it to a boil again for 1 minute.

PRESERVE

See pages 29–30 for in-depth instructions on filling and processing the jars.

For this recipe, process the jars in a boiling water bath for 6 minutes.

TIPS

Pairs well with creamy, sweet, and tangy fresh ricotta or *burrata*; great in a tart with fresh cream; delicious on top of ice cream or yogurt. See Make It Your Own on pages 82–83 for unique flavor combinations and ingredients you can use to customize your own flavor.

APRICOT JAM

| With fresh thyme and vanilla—richly hued apricots are enhanced with savory and mellow notes |

Apricots are vibrantly orange-colored fruits; in the Northeast, they're a harbinger of stone fruit season—other stone fruits are peaches, plums, and nectarines. Fresh apricots are a delight! They're full of healthy beta-carotene, fiber, and vitamin C, and are in season in North America from May through August. If you see them in the grocery store during the winter, they've probably been shipped from South America or New Zealand.

Related to peaches and plums, apricots have velvety skin and soft flesh. They are not too juicy but are pleasurably smooth, sweet, and richly tangy. Their flavor is delicately musky, with a slight tartness that lies somewhere in between a peach and a plum.

Adding a fresh herb like thyme and a smooth spice such as vanilla deepens the flavor and adds a fresh edge to this jam. Apricots are easy to make into jam—they practically jam themselves—and leaving the skins on adds a nice tartness.

You can do the first day's steps in this recipe in ten minutes when you get back from the market or grocery store with your fruit. The next day it will take you about forty minutes to cook the jam and process the jars.

Makes About Four 8-Ounce Jars or Twot Pint Jars

INGREDIENTS
3 pounds apricots (about 9 cups)
3 cups sugar (1½ pounds)
7 ounces water
3 tablespoons lemon juice
10 sprigs of thyme
1 vanilla bean

Special Equipment
1 candy thermometer
1 chinois sieve

PREP

For the apricots:

Rinse the apricots and quarter, leaving the skin on and discarding the pits. Measure the fruit into a glass bowl or a plastic food-safe Tupperware container and add the sugar, water, lemon juice, and thyme. Split and scrape the vanilla bean into the mixture, adding the bean pod as well.

Stir well. Refrigerate or leave in a cool place overnight or up to 24 hours so that the sugar and lemon juice are allowed to release the juice of the apricots. Stir every so often to dissolve the sugar.

The next day, drain this mixture through a fine sieve. Place the collected syrup in a 6- to 8-quart nonreactive pot. Reserve the fruit.

For the jars and lids:

Wash and rinse the jars; put them into a big stockpot; cover the jars with water and bring to a boil; turn off the heat. Let stand in hot water until you are ready to fill.

Bring the lids and rings to a boil; turn off the heat. Let stand in hot water until you are ready to screw them onto the jars.

Place a few metal spoons in the freezer for testing the consistency and gel of your jam later. You can also place them in a cup of ice water, if you prefer.

COOK

Bring the collected syrup to a boil over high heat. Skim and continue cooking on high heat, stirring frequently to prevent scorching. The syrup will reach the gel stage at 221°F (105°C) on a candy thermometer, about 10 minutes. If you don't have a thermometer, test the consistency by placing a teaspoon of the hot jam onto one of the prepped frozen spoons. Let it rest for a few minutes, then test the gel by tilting the spoon vertically. What is the consistency? If the jam runs loosely like syrup, bring it to a boil again for 1 to 5 minutes. Add the apricot quarters, discarding the thyme and vanilla. Boil for 5 minutes, stirring gently to prevent scorching. Skim any foam that surfaces. Check the set with a prepped cold spoon, as you did with the syrup. It should be firm and glide slowly down the spoon.

Once it is done, turn off the heat.

PRESERVE

See pages 29–30 for in-depth instructions on filling and processing the jars.

For this recipe, process the jars in a boiling water bath for 6 minutes.

TIPS

Pairs well with soft cheese such as Camembert and Coupole or with bloomy and buttery Humboldt Fog cheese; great on sourdough toast or scones; delicious on top of yogurt or creamy desserts such as *panna cotta* (recipe on page 233). See Make It Your Own on pages 82–83 for unique flavor combinations and ingredients you can use to customize your own flavor.

SUGAR PLUM FAIRY JAM

| *With ice wine—small heirloom plums with their tart skin are anointed with the ambrosia of ice wine* |

Farmers' markets often refer to a variety of early, small plums as sugar plums, but that's just a generic name for sweet and small early plums. My favorites are Blackamber, Elephant Heart, Myrobalan (or cherry plums), Mirabelle, or Greengage. I love making this jam with golden plums like Mirabelle or Myrobalan—they create a jam that's a beautiful glowing yellow color.

In this recipe, ice wine adds a sweet, rich flavor. Ice wine is lovely—an ambrosia elixir. The grapes are left on the vine long after harvest time, and on the coldest moment of a winter's night, when temperatures are below 15°F, the vintners trudge through the snow to pick the frozen grapes. In its frozen state, each grape produces just a few drops of sweet juice that's released and fermented. The Pacific Northwest is a great area for ice wine, but New York State produces delicious ice wine, too, particularly from the Finger Lakes region.

If you're feeling fancy, use my favorite variation, a Trockenbeerenauslese (translation: "select dried berries"), which is an intensely sweet dessert wine from Austria that's made from grapes that are allowed to shrivel up like raisins and develop a dry "noble rot." They have an intensely rich flavor, with notes of caramel, honey, and apricot.

You can increase the alcohol ratio in this recipe with a tablespoon more of ice wine if you fancy a more boozy jam. This is a tart jam; if you want to add more sweetness, test the flavor while cooking and add another half cup of sugar.

This jam is a two-day process, but day one is simple. If you want to do it in one day, allow the plums to macerate for a few hours at room temperature, and they should render enough juice for the recipe.

Makes About Four 8-Ounce Jars or Two Pint Jars

INGREDIENTS
2 pounds plums (about 5 cups)
2 cups sugar (1 pound)
3 tablespoons lemon juice
1 cup ice wine

SPECIAL EQUIPMENT
1 candy thermometer

PREP

FOR THE PLUMS:

Rinse the plums and halve, leaving the skin on and discarding the pits. Measure the fruit into a glass bowl or plastic food-safe Tupperware container and add the sugar and lemon juice.

Stir well. Macerate at room temperature for 1 hour, stir to help dissolve the sugar, then refrigerate or leave in a cool place overnight or up to 24 hours so that the sugar and lemon juice are allowed to release the juice of the plums.

The next day, place the plums and all their juice in a 6- to 8-quart nonreactive pot.

FOR THE JARS AND LIDS:

Wash and rinse the jars; put them into a big stockpot; cover the jars with water and bring to a boil; turn off the heat. Let stand in hot water until ready to fill.

Bring the lids and rings to a boil; turn off the heat. Let stand in hot water until ready to screw them onto the jars.

Place a few metal spoons in the freezer for testing the consistency and gel of your jam later. You can also place them in a cup of ice water, if you prefer.

COOK

Bring the plums to a boil on high heat and continue cooking for 5 minutes. Skim and continue cooking on high heat, stirring frequently to prevent scorching.

Add the ice wine and return to a boil for another 5 minutes. Skim and return to a boil. The syrup will reach the gel stage at 221°F (105°C) on a candy thermometer, about 10 more minutes. If you don't have a thermometer, test the consistency by placing a teaspoon of the hot jam onto one of the prepped frozen spoons. Let it rest for a few minutes, then test the gel by tilting the spoon vertically. What is the consistency? If the jam runs loosely like syrup then it's not done yet, but if it glides slowly along in a gloopy glob, then the jam is ready. If syrupy, bring it to a boil again for 1 to 5 minutes.

Once it is done, turn off the heat.

PRESERVE

See pages 29–30 for in-depth instructions on filling and processing the jars.

For this recipe, process the jars in a boiling water bath for 6 minutes.

TIPS

Pairs well with bloomy and buttery Crottin or hard and snappy Vieille; great on olive oil crackers or sage salami; delicious on top of yogurt or creamy desserts. See Make It Your Own on pages 82–83 for unique flavor combinations and ingredients you can use to customize your own flavor.

REALLY ROSIE JAM

| *Ethereal golden raspberries—enhance their delicate floral flavor with rosewater* |

The name of the jam is a nod to one of my childhood heroes, Really Rosie. She was the sassy heroine of the musical by Maurice Sendak and Carole King, and I used to carry the cassette tape along with me in the car when I was a kid and sing along.

Golden raspberries can be the most incredible tasting fruit if you get them at peak ripeness and make this jam right away. Rosewater adds an unusual botanic note to the tart berries and enhances their subtle flavor. You can substitute red raspberries for the golden, if you must.

Makes About Four 8-Ounce Jars or Two Pint Jars

INGREDIENTS

2¼ pounds golden raspberries (about 8 cups)
2 cups sugar (1 pound)
3 tablespoons lemon juice
3 tablespoons rosewater

For the Gelling

See Chapter 3 for more information on pectin and calcium water
5 teaspoons calcium water
4 teaspoons pectin

PREP

For the raspberries:

Gently rinse the berries and remove any stems. Measure the fruit into a 6- to 8-quart nonreactive pot and add the lemon juice and the proper amount of calcium water into the pan; stir well.

For the jars and lids:

Wash and rinse the jars; put them into a big stockpot; cover the jars with water and bring to a boil; turn off the heat. Let stand in hot water until ready to fill.

Bring the lids and rings to a boil; turn off the heat. Let stand in hot water until ready to screw them onto the jars.

Place a few metal spoons in the freezer for testing the consistency and gel of your jam later. You can also place them in a cup of ice water, if you prefer.

For the sugar and pectin:

Measure the sugar into a separate bowl or measuring cup and thoroughly mix the proper amount of pectin powder into the sugar—using a fork helps to disperse the pectin into the sugar. Set the sugar mixture aside.

COOK

Bring the fruit to a boil over medium-high heat. If it starts to foam, skim the foam off the top and discard the foam. Add the rosewater and return to a boil.

Pour the pectin-sugar mixture into the boiling jam slowly and carefully, stirring as you add. Stir vigorously 1 to 2 minutes to dissolve the pectin.

Return the fruit to a boil and remove from the heat. Skim off any and all foam that has formed on the top.

Pectin gels completely when thoroughly cool, so don't worry if your jam looks loose while still hot. To test, place a teaspoon of the hot jam onto one of the prepped frozen spoons; let it cool to room temperature (about 30 seconds) on the spoon. If it thickens up to the consistency desired, then the jam is ready. If not, mix in a little more pectin (½ teaspoon into ¼ cup sugar) and bring it to a boil again for 1 minute.

PRESERVE

See pages 29–30 for in-depth instructions on filling and processing the jars.

For this recipe, process the jars in a boiling water bath for 6 minutes.

TIPS

Pairs well with fresh cheeses like chèvre and fresh ricotta; great on scones with clotted cream (recipe on page 205); delicious on top of ice cream or yogurt. See Make It Your Own on pages 82–83 for unique flavor combinations and ingredients you can use to customize your own flavor.

THAI ME UP JAM

| *Nectarines get a Southeast Asian twist with ginger and Kaffir lime leaves* |

The patterns on white nectarines are so beautiful—like an Impressionist painting or the blush on a woman's pale cheek—that it can be difficult to cut them up and cook them, but you'll see it's well worth it once you taste this jam.

Kaffir lime leaves add an exotic citrus note to the sweet and mellow nectarines. I first discovered Kaffir limes when I was traveling in Thailand and Indonesia. In Thailand they are used in the dish *tom yum*. I can still taste the tart and sour flavor of the leaves on my tongue as I drank the spicy soup to cool me down during a hot summer in the Gulf of Thailand. My friends from Jakarta, Indonesia, taught me to use them in *sayur asam*, a vegetable soup with tamarind and peanuts. They have a unique flavor. Use fresh or frozen leaves, but not dried leaves because most of the flavor will be lost. See "Sources" on page 250 for information on where to purchase them.

Makes About Four 8-Ounce Jars or Two Pint Jars

INGREDIENTS
2 pounds white nectarines (about 5 cups)
4 Kaffir lime leaves
2 tablespoons lemon juice
1 ounce finely chopped fresh ginger
2 cups sugar (1 pound)

For the Gelling
See Chapter 3 for more information on pectin and calcium water
3 teaspoons calcium water
2 teaspoons pectin

Special Equipment
1 piece cheesecloth

PREP
For the nectarines:
Blanch the nectarines in a pot of boiling water for about 1 minute. Refresh them by plunging them in an ice water bath and leaving them there for at least 30 seconds;

this will help loosen the peel and you should be able to easily pull it off with your hands. Roughly chop the nectarines and remove their pits.

Bruise the Kaffir lime leaves by pounding on them with the back of a paring knife for a few seconds each; tie them up in a piece of cheesecloth.

Measure the fruit into a glass bowl or plastic food-safe Tupperware container and add the lemon juice, ginger, 1 cup sugar, and Kaffir lime leaves in the cheesecloth. Stir well. Let them macerate at room temperature for a few hours, until the sugar and lemon juice are allowed to release the juice of the fruit. Stir every once in a while to dissolve the sugar.

Once the juice is released, place the fruit into a 6- to 8-quart nonreactive pot and add the proper amount of calcium water into the pan; stir well.

FOR THE JARS AND LIDS:
Wash and rinse the jars; put them into a big stockpot; cover the jars with water and bring to a boil; turn off the heat. Let stand in hot water until you are ready to fill.

Bring the lids and rings to a boil; turn off the heat. Let stand in hot water until you are ready to screw them onto the jars.

Place a few metal spoons in the freezer for testing the consistency and gel of your jam later. You can also place them in a cup of ice water, if you prefer.

FOR THE SUGAR AND PECTIN:

Measure the remaining 1 cup sugar into a separate bowl or measuring cup and thoroughly mix the proper amount of pectin powder into the sugar—using a fork helps to disperse the pectin into the sugar. Set the sugar mixture aside.

COOK

Bring the fruit to a boil over medium-high heat. If it starts to foam, skim the foam off the top and discard the foam. Remove the Kaffir lime leaves in cheesecloth.

Pour the pectin-sugar mixture into the boiling jam slowly and carefully, stirring as you add. Stir vigorously for 1 to 2 minutes to dissolve the pectin.

Return the fruit to a boil and remove from the heat. Skim off any and all foam that has formed on the top. Pectin gels completely when thoroughly cool, so don't worry if your jam looks loose while still hot. To test, place a teaspoon of the hot jam onto one of the prepped frozen spoons; let it cool to room temperature (about 30 seconds) on the spoon. If it thickens up to the consistency desired, then the jam is ready. If not, mix in a little more pectin (½ teaspoon into ¼ cup sugar) and bring it to a boil again for 1 minute.

PRESERVE

See pages 29–30 for in-depth instructions on filling and processing the jars.

For this recipe, process the jars in a boiling water bath for 6 minutes.

TIPS

Pairs well with hard, caramelly cheese such as Mimolette and aged goat Gouda; great with grilled fish; delicious on top of cold creamy desserts like ice cream or crème caramel. See Make It Your Own on pages 82–83 for unique flavor combinations and ingredients you can use to customize your own flavor.

WILD BLUEBERRY JAM

| *Intensely flavorful wild blueberries from Maine are spiced up with rum, juniper, and anise* |

On a wild and rainy summer night, I pulled up to the curb and met a man at the Bowery Hotel, where I slipped him an unmarked envelope of cash. After a brief exchange under the awning that shrouded us from the street and a perpetual veil of rain, I left with my reward, fleeing into the street, into the night, over the Williamsburg Bridge, and back to Brooklyn. I stashed what I'd bought in the refrigerator, wedged beside peaches and apples to await their fate.

Wild blueberries are such divine contraband! The man I'd met at the Bowery Hotel was Doug, a handsome and skilled farmer who harvests organic wild blueberries at Continuous Harmony Farm. The farm is nestled in some of the prettiest countryside you can imagine up in Lincolnville, a town on the coast of Maine. I use them in this jam to showcase their delicious and tart blueberriness.

This is an adult jam, perfect for those with riper palettes who like dark rum and unusual anise and juniper flavors.

Makes About Six 8-Ounce Jars or Three Pint Jars

INGREDIENTS
2 pounds wild blueberries (about 6 cups)
5 juniper berries, fresh if possible
4 star anise
3 cups sugar (1½ pounds)
2 tablespoons lemon juice
2 ounces dark rum

For the Gelling
See Chapter 3 for more information on pectin and calcium water
4 teaspoons calcium water
3 teaspoons pectin

Special Equipment
1 piece cheesecloth

PREP

FOR THE BLUEBERRIES:

Rinse the blueberries and remove their stems. Tie the juniper berries and star anise in a cheesecloth. Measure the fruit into a glass bowl or plastic food-safe Tupperware container and add 1 cup sugar, the lemon juice, and juniper berries and star anise tied up in cheesecloth. Stir well. Let macerate at room temperature for a few hours or overnight, until the sugar and lemon juice are allowed to release the juice of the fruit. Stir every once in a while to dissolve the sugar.

Once the juice is released, place the fruit and spices in their cheesecloth into a 6- to 8-quart nonreactive pot and add the proper amount of calcium water into the pan; stir well.

FOR THE JARS AND LIDS:

Wash and rinse the jars; put them into a big stockpot; cover the jars with water and bring to a boil; turn off the heat. Let stand in hot water until you are ready to fill.

Bring the lids and rings to a boil; turn off the heat. Let stand in hot water until you are ready to screw them onto the jars.

Place a few metal spoons in the freezer for testing the consistency and gel of your jam later. You can also place them in a cup of ice water, if you prefer.

FOR THE SUGAR AND PECTIN:

Measure the remaining 2 cups sugar into a separate bowl or measuring cup and thoroughly mix the proper amount of pectin powder into the sugar—using a fork helps to disperse the pectin into the sugar. Set the sugar mixture aside.

COOK

Bring the fruit to a boil over medium-high heat. If it starts to foam, skim the foam off the top and discard the foam. Remove the juniper and star anise in cheesecloth and add the rum. Return the fruit to a boil.

Pour the pectin-sugar mixture into the boiling jam slowly and carefully, stirring as you add. Stir vigorously for 1 to 2 minutes to dissolve the pectin.

Return the fruit to a boil and remove from the heat. Skim off any and all foam that has formed on the top.

Pectin gels completely when thoroughly cool, so don't worry if your jam looks loose while still hot. To test, place a teaspoon of the hot jam onto one of the prepped frozen spoons; let it cool to room temperature (about 30 seconds) on the spoon. If it thickens up to the consistency desired, then the jam is ready. If not, mix in a little more pectin (½ teaspoon into ¼ cup sugar) and bring it to a boil again for 1 minute.

PRESERVE

See pages 29–30 for in-depth instructions on filling and processing the jars.

For this recipe, process the jars in a boiling water bath for 6 minutes.

TIPS

Pairs well with mild, fresh cheeses such as fresh ricotta and *burrata*; great on French toast or pancakes; delicious on top of ice cream or thick Greek yogurt. See Make It Your Own on pages 82–83 for unique flavor combinations and ingredients you can use to customize your own flavor.

HOT FIREMAN'S PEAR JAM

| *With warm chipotle and cinnamon—a perfect autumn jam to make during pear season* |

When I invented this jam a few years ago, I used pears from a fireman who also happens to have a small pear farm in Accord, New York. The word *hot* in the title references both the spicy dried chilies in the jam and the sexy reputation of firemen. The original pear-farmer/fireman is not as young as he used to be and not the quintessential "hot fireman," but he still gets a kick out of the name of this jam.

Pears are a great fruit to preserve, as their flavor becomes sweeter and their texture turns buttery when they're cooked. And they taste great with a variety of herbs and spices. Chipotle peppers are smoke-dried jalapeño peppers that are used in Mexican and Tex-Mex cuisine. They have a medium heat and won't hurt like a habanero or other superhot chili.

In this recipe, the spices are not meant to burn your tongue off, but to enhance the flavor of the pears and warm the taste buds. It's a slow-burn sensation, so you taste the smokiness and spiciness of the chipotle after you taste the sweetness of the pears. Feel free to add more chipotle powder if you like it hot.

Pairing pears with cheese is a classic combination. Or try it on PB&J, as my friends at SlantShack Jerky, makers of artisanal beef jerky, like to do.

Makes About Four 8-Ounce Jars or Two Pint Jars

INGREDIENTS

2 pounds pears (about 5 cups or 6 medium pears)
½ cup water
2 tablespoons lemon juice
2 cups sugar (1 pound)
2 teaspoons chipotle powder
2 teaspoons ground cinnamon

FOR THE GELLING

See Chapter 3 for more information on pectin and calcium water
3 teaspoons calcium water
2 teaspoons pectin

Special Equipment
1 potato masher

PREP

For the pears:

Rinse, peel, core, and dice the pears. Measure the fruit into a 6- to 8-quart nonreactive pot, add the ½ cup water, lemon juice, and the appropriate amount of calcium water into the pan; stir well.

For the jars and lids:

Wash and rinse the jars; put them into a big stockpot; cover the jars with water and bring to a boil; turn off the heat. Let stand in hot water until you are ready to fill.

Bring the lids and rings to a boil; turn off the heat. Let stand in hot water until you are ready to screw them onto the jars.

Place a few metal spoons in the freezer for testing the consistency and gel of your jam later. You can also place them in a cup of ice water, if you prefer.

For the sugar and pectin:

Measure the sugar into a separate bowl or measuring cup and thoroughly mix the proper amount of pectin powder into the sugar—using a fork helps to disperse the pectin into the sugar. Set the sugar mixture aside.

COOK

Bring the pears to a boil over medium-high heat, cover them with a lid, and cook for 30 minutes, until the pears begin to appear translucent. Remove the cover and add the chipotle powder and cinnamon.

Mash the fruit with a potato masher until most of the fruit chunks have been broken apart. Do not mash into a smooth consistency; allow for a variety of sizes and textures in the fruit.

Return the pears to a boil and stir frequently to prevent scorching.

Pour the pectin-sugar mixture into the boiling jam slowly and carefully, stirring as you add. Stir vigorously 1 to 2 minutes to dissolve the pectin.

Return the fruit to a boil and remove from the heat. Skim off any and all foam that has formed on the top.

Pectin gels completely when thoroughly cool, so don't worry if your jam looks loose while still hot. To test, place a teaspoon of the hot jam onto one of the prepped frozen spoons; let it cool to room temperature (about 30 seconds) on the spoon. If it thickens up to the consistency desired, then the jam is ready. If not, mix in a little more pectin (½ teaspoon into ¼ cup sugar) and bring it to a boil again for 1 minute.

PRESERVE

See pages 29–30 for in-depth instructions on filling and processing the jars.

For this recipe, process the jars in a boiling water bath for 6 minutes.

TIPS

Pairs well with soft cheese such as Coupole and La Tur; great on grilled cheese with fontina (see recipe on page 211); delicious on sandwiches with duck rillettes or sage salami. See Make It Your Own on pages 82–83 for unique flavor combinations and ingredients you can use to customize your own flavor.

FIGALICIOUS JAM

| *With just a touch of vanilla bean and blood orange juice—a divine, pure, and perfect fig jam* |

The scent of fig trees—musky, damp, sweet, and earthy—immediately transports me to childhood summers in Greece. There was a mountain path I used to walk down on the island of Andros that was covered with fig trees. It was September and the second fig crop of the year was ripe. Everywhere you went, there was the scent of figs overhead—all you had to do was reach up and pluck them down into your mouth. I often had a stomachache—eating them was too hard to resist.

You can find good figs that will work in this jam in many parts of the United States during early and late autumn. For this recipe, use the ripest ones you can find; a ripe fig is soft, juicy, and oozing. Figs are like tomatoes in that their pH level can hover near the danger zone of 4.6 (see "Basics" on page 18 for more information about pH levels). This means you have to add citrus juice to make them safe to process in a water bath, and you'll notice that you have to process them for longer than most other jam recipes in this book.

This jam takes two days from start to finish, but it's actually pretty simple. You can do the prep work on the first day in ten minutes when you get back from the market or grocery store with your figs. The next day it will take about an hour to cook the jam and process the jars.

Makes About Four 8-Ounce Jars or Two Pint Jars

INGREDIENTS

2 pounds figs (about 5 cups)
3 cups sugar (1½ pounds)
2 blood oranges, juiced (about 6 tablespoons)
3 tablespoons lemon juice
1 vanilla bean

Special Equipment
1 candy thermometer

PREP

For the figs:
Rinse the figs and dry gently in a towel. Remove the stems and slice the figs in halves. Measure the fruit into a glass bowl or plastic food-safe Tupperware container

and add the sugar, blood orange juice, and lemon juice. Split and scrape the vanilla bean into the mixture, adding the bean pod as well.

Stir well. Macerate at room temperature for 1 hour, stir to help dissolve the sugar, then refrigerate or leave in a cool place overnight or up to 24 hours so that the sugar and lemon juice are allowed to macerate the figs.

The next day, place this preparation in a 6- to 8-quart nonreactive pot.

FOR THE JARS AND LIDS:

Wash and rinse the jars; put them into a big stockpot; cover the jars with water and bring to a boil; turn off the heat. Let stand in hot water until you are ready to fill.

Bring the lids and rings to a boil; turn off the heat. Let stand in hot water until you are ready to screw them onto the jars.

Place a few metal spoons in the freezer for testing the consistency and gel of your jam later. You can also place them in a cup of ice water, if you prefer.

COOK

Bring the figs to a boil over high heat and continue cooking for 5 to 10 minutes. Skim and return to a boil, stirring gently. The jam will reach the gel stage at 221°F (105°C) on a candy thermometer, 5 to 10 more minutes. If you don't have a thermometer, test the consistency by placing a teaspoon of the hot jam onto one of the prepped frozen spoons. Let it rest for a few minutes, then test the gel by tilting the spoon vertically. What is the consistency? If the jam runs loosely like syrup then it's not done yet, but if it glides slowly along in a gloopy glob, then the jam is ready. If syrupy, bring it to a boil again for 1 to 5 minutes.

Once it is done, turn off the heat.

PRESERVE

See pages 29–30 for in-depth instructions on filling and processing the jars.

Since figs are lower in acid than most fruit, process the jars in a boiling water bath for 12 minutes.

TIPS

Pairs well with creamy and intense goat cheeses such as Selles-sur-Cher, Chevrot, or La Tur, and pairs equally well with Manchego; great in tarts; delicious on a pizza with prosciutto, arugula, Parmesan, and Gorgonzola, and a drizzle of truffle oil (see recipe on page 219). See Make It Your Own on pages 82–83 for unique flavor combinations and ingredients you can use to customize your own flavor.

WATERMELON AND LEMONGRASS JELLY

| Cool and refreshing watermelon gets a twist with lemongrass |

Watermelons are the essence of summer, and people who dislike them are usually turned off by the watery, grainy texture. Turning watermelon into jelly is a great way to circumvent the texture and still taste the delicious flavor.

My neighbors at New Amsterdam Market at the South Street Seaport are a lovely family with a farm in New Jersey called Z Food Farm. They're the nicest folks and generously ply my staff and me with gorgeous and delicious certified-organic veggies.

This summer they gave me a ginormous twenty-seven-pound watermelon to use for jelly. They also had some amazing lemongrass that paired perfectly with the melon for a superrefreshing jelly. I was surprised that lemongrass could grow in this climate, but it tasted great. If you don't have an awesome farmer to supply you with local lemongrass, you can often find it at Asian grocery stores or bigger gourmet stores like Whole Foods Market.

This jelly has the most amazing color: bright orangey-pink like a Jolly Rancher candy. It's fun and will appeal to kids, while at the same time it has a unique and complex flavor that will appeal to the most discerning adult. It has a diverse range of fans whom I sell it to at the markets, from ten-year-old sisters to a male fashion designer.

Makes About Four 8-Ounce Jars or Two Pint Jars

INGREDIENTS

1 medium watermelon (4 cups watermelon pulp)
3 stalks lemongrass
3 tablespoons lemon juice
2 cups sugar (1 pound), or more to taste
½ teaspoon salt

FOR THE GELLING

See Chapter 3 for more information on pectin and calcium water
3 teaspoons calcium water
2 teaspoons pectin

1 sieve, food mill, or juicer

PREP

FOR THE WATERMELON AND LEMONGRASS:
Halve the watermelon and scoop out the flesh. Press the mixture through a sieve or use a food mill or juicer to separate the pulp from the seeds and smooth the texture. Bruise the lemongrass stalks by beating with a meat mallet or the back of a knife; if the stalks are too long to fit in the pot, cut them in half or bend them and tie in a knot. Measure the watermelon pulp and lemongrass stalks into a 6- to 8-quart nonreactive pot and add lemon juice, salt, and the proper amount of calcium water into the pan; stir well.

FOR THE JARS AND LIDS:
Wash and rinse the jars; put them into a big stockpot; cover the jars with water and bring to a boil; turn off the heat. Let stand in hot water until you are ready to fill.

Bring the lids and rings to a boil; turn off the heat. Let stand in hot water until you are ready to screw them onto the jars.

Place a few metal spoons in the freezer for testing the consistency and gel of your jam later. You can also place them in a cup of ice water, if you prefer.

FOR THE SUGAR AND PECTIN:
Measure the sugar into a separate bowl or measuring cup and thoroughly mix the proper amount of pectin powder into the sugar—using a fork helps to disperse the pectin into the sugar. Set the sugar mixture aside.

COOK

Bring the fruit to a boil. If it starts to foam, skim the foam off the top and discard the foam. Remove the lemongrass.

Pour the pectin-sugar mixture into the boiling jelly slowly and carefully, stirring as you add. Stir vigorously 1 to 2 minutes to dissolve the pectin. Taste for sweetness and add ¼ cup more sugar if it's too tart for your liking.

Return the fruit to a boil over high heat and remove from the heat. Skim off any and all foam that has formed on the top.

Pectin gels completely when thoroughly cool, so don't worry if your jelly looks loose when still hot. To test, place a teaspoon of the hot jelly onto one of the prepped frozen spoons; let it cool to room temperature (about 30 seconds) on the spoon. If it thickens up to the consistency desired, then the jelly is ready. If not, mix in a little more pectin (½ teaspoon into ¼ cup sugar) and bring it to a boil again for 1 minute.

PRESERVE

See pages 29–30 for in-depth instructions on filling and processing the jars.

For this recipe, process the jars in a boiling water bath for 6 minutes.

TIPS

Pairs well with bloomy and stinky cheeses such as Crottin or Cowgirl Creamery Mt. Tam, and washed-rind taleggio; great on buttery sourdough toast; delicious on top of ice cream or yogurt. See Make It Your Own on pages 82–83 for unique flavor combinations and ingredients you can use to customize your own flavor.

FINGER LAKES WINE GRAPE JELLY

| *Grape jelly turns wild with grapes from upstate New York's wine region* |

Grape jelly has a bad reputation. It conjures little plastic packets served with toast at a diner, or cloyingly sweet jelly that barely resembles real grapes and is chock-full of preservatives and coloring. . . . But I encourage you to give grape jelly another try!

In late summer, a few farmers bring unusual grapes to the markets in New York City. Many are wine grapes from the Finger Lakes wine country in upstate New York, and their flavor is amazing for jelly. Norton and Cabernet Franc pomace are common in many parts of the United States and are fun grapes to use for this recipe. If you live in California or another wine-rich area, then lucky you—it should be easy to find great grapes to play with and develop your own version. You can call the recipe Central Valley Wine Grape Jelly if you're in Southern California or Willamette Valley Wine Grape Jelly if you're in Oregon.

Although not wine grapes, Muscadine and Concord grapes are great to use, too, if you can't find wine grapes.

Makes About Four 8-Ounce Jars or Two Pint Jars

INGREDIENTS

2¾ pounds grapes (½ gallon or 8 cups)
3 tablespoons lemon juice
2 cups sugar (1 pound), or more to taste

For the Gelling

See Chapter 3 for more information on pectin and calcium water
3 teaspoons calcium water
2 teaspoons pectin

Special Equipment

1 potato masher
1 sieve or food mill

PREP

FOR THE GRAPES:

Rinse the grapes well and remove the stems. Place the grapes in a 6- to 8-quart nonreactive pot; add water to cover, just until the grapes start to float, about 4 cups. Cover with a lid and bring to a boil over medium-high heat. Reduce the heat to medium and cook until the grapes are soft, 30 to 40 minutes.

When the grapes appear soft and slightly wrinkled, mash them using a potato masher. Press the mixture through a sieve or use a food mill to separate the pulp from the skins and seeds. Make sure to scrape any excess pulp from underneath the sieve into the bowl. Transfer the grape pulp and juice into a 6- to 8-quart nonreactive pot. Add lemon juice and the proper amount of calcium water into the pan; stir well.

FOR THE JARS AND LIDS:

Wash and rinse the jars; put them into a big stockpot; cover the jars with water and bring to a boil; turn off the heat. Let stand in hot water until you are ready to fill.

Bring the lids and rings to a boil; turn off the heat. Let stand in hot water until you are ready to screw them onto the jars.

Place a few metal spoons in the freezer for testing the consistency and gel of your jam later. You can also place them in a cup of ice water, if you prefer.

FOR THE SUGAR AND PECTIN:

Measure the sugar into a separate bowl or measuring cup and thoroughly mix the proper amount of pectin powder into the sugar—using a fork helps to disperse the pectin into the sugar. Set the sugar mixture aside.

COOK

Bring the fruit to a boil over medium-high heat. If it starts to foam, skim the foam off the top and discard the foam. Return to a boil.

Pour the pectin-sugar mixture into the boiling jelly slowly and carefully, stirring as you add. Stir vigorously for 1 to 2 minutes to dissolve the pectin. Taste for sweetness and add ¼ cup more sugar if it's too tart for your liking.

Return the fruit to a boil and remove from the heat. Skim off any and all foam that has formed on the top.

Pectin gels completely when thoroughly cool, so don't worry if your jelly looks loose while still hot. To test, place a teaspoon of the hot jelly onto one of the prepped frozen spoons; let it cool to room temperature (about 30 seconds) on the spoon. If it thickens up to the consistency desired, then the jelly is ready. If not, mix in a little more pectin (½ teaspoon into ¼ cup sugar) and bring it to a boil again for 1 minute.

PRESERVE

See pages 29–30 for in-depth instructions on filling and processing the jars.

For this recipe, process the jars in a boiling water bath for 6 minutes.

TIPS

Pairs well with bloomy and buttery cheeses such as Cremont and Bucheron; great on a hot dog with ketchup and mayo, crushed pineapple, and potato chips (a big winner in the Great Hotdog Cookoff of 2009); delicious on a PB&J with almond butter and whole-wheat bread. See Make It Your Own on pages 82–83 for unique flavor combinations and ingredients you can use to customize your own flavor.

SPICED BEER JELLY

| *With beer, apples, and spices—a delicious apple jelly base is infused*
with a hint of malt and hops |

While doing some jam research, I happened upon a few mentions of ale jelly in historical cookbooks. The cookery column of *The Queen* newspaper in the United Kingdom had a recipe in 1902 that called for good beer "not bitter" and *The Economics of Modern Cookery; Or, A Younger Son's Cookery Book* had a similar recipe for ale jelly, described as "very good—much better than it sounds." The recipes gave vague instructions to cook ale, lemon, and sugar together. I found a more modern version in Christine Ferber's *Mes Confitures* that was much easier to adapt. Apples are the fruit base and make for a delicious jelly.

For my version of this recipe for my business, I always buy my beer from a local brewery in Brooklyn called Sixpoint Craft Ales. Sixpoint, run by Shane Welch, has brought brewing back to New York City, operating one of the only microbreweries in the region. Until the mid-1960s, Brooklyn produced one-fifth of the nation's beer.

Sixpoint's beautifully handcrafted beers, and the love and attention they put into their craft, are a fitting part of the creative renaissance in Brooklyn over the past few years. Brewing beer is similar in some ways to jam making, particularly Sixpoint's creative use of herbs, spices, and local produce. I recently stopped by the Sixpoint brewery and found head brewer Ian McConnell knee-deep in Concord grapes as he experimented with a grape-infused beer.

I use a different beer for each season when I make this recipe. During the summer, I use Vienna Pale Ale, which has a nice light golden mouthfeel; in fall, I use Brownstoner, which tastes nutty and yeasty, with nice coffee and chocolate· undertones; and in winter I often use a cranberry-infused porter. When choosing the type of beer to use, the less bitter the beer, the better, since the bitter hops can ruin the flavor. The flavor will change a lot depending on the beer, so I recommend experimenting with your favorite local beers and finding one that's unique to you.

Makes About Five 8-Ounce Jars

INGREDIENTS
2 pounds flavorful apples, such as Cortland or Stayman Winesap
5¼ cups sugar (about 2½ pounds), or more to taste
3 cups dark beer (about two 12-ounce bottles)

3 tablespoons lemon juice (about 2 small lemons)
2 sticks of cinnamon
¼ teaspoon ground Grains of Paradise
¼ teaspoon ground black cardamom

For the Gelling
See Chapter 3 for more information on pectin and calcium water
2½ teaspoons pectin
3 teaspoons calcium water

Special Equipment
1 chinois sieve or jelly bag

PREP

For the apples:

Rinse the apples in cold water. Stem and cut the apples into quarters without peeling or coring them.

Place the apples in a 6- to 8-quart nonreactive pot and cover with water. Bring them to a boil over medium-high heat, reduce the heat, and allow them to simmer for 30 minutes on low heat until the apples are soft.

Collect the juice made by the apples by pouring this preparation through a fine chinois sieve or jelly bag and pressing lightly on the fruit. Let the juice drain out completely so you have the proper 2½ cups, preferably overnight in the refrigerator.

For the jars and lids:

Wash and rinse the jars; put them into a big stockpot; cover the jars with water and bring to a boil; turn off the heat. Let stand in hot water until you are ready to fill.

Bring the lids and rings to a boil; turn off the heat. Let stand in hot water until you are ready to screw them onto the jars.

Place a few metal spoons in the freezer for testing the consistency and gel of your jam later. You can also place them in a cup of ice water, if you prefer.

For the sugar and pectin:

The next day, measure 1 cup sugar into a separate bowl or measuring cup and thoroughly mix the proper amount of pectin powder into the sugar—using a fork helps to disperse the pectin into the sugar. Set the sugar mixture aside.

COOK

The next day, measure 2½ cups of the apple juice, leaving and discarding any residue that settled at the bottom overnight. Pour the apple juice, beer, remaining 4¼ cups sugar, lemon juice, cinnamon sticks, Grains of Paradise, and black cardamom into a 6- to 8-quart Dutch oven or a stainless-steel or copper pot and add the proper amount of calcium water into the pan; stir well. Bring to a simmer.

Skim carefully if there is any foam and continue cooking on high heat for 10 to 15 minutes, stirring gently. Skim again, if necessary. Remove the cinnamon sticks and return to a boil.

Pour the pectin-sugar mixture into the boiling jelly slowly and carefully, stirring as you add. Stir vigorously for 1 to 2 minutes to dissolve the pectin. Taste for sweetness and add ¼ cup more sugar if it's too tart for your liking.

Return the fruit to a boil and remove from the heat. Skim off any and all foam that has formed on the top.

Pectin gels completely when thoroughly cool, so don't worry if your jelly looks loose while still hot. To test, place a teaspoon of the hot jelly onto one of the prepped frozen spoons; let it cool to room temperature (about 30 seconds) on the spoon. If it thickens up to the consistency desired, then the jelly is ready. If not, mix in a little more pectin (½ teaspoon into ¼ cup sugar) and bring it to a boil again for 1 minute.

PRESERVE

See pages 29–30 for in-depth instructions on filling and processing the jars.

For this recipe, process the jars in a boiling water bath for 6 minutes.

TIPS

Pairs well with semisoft Tomme de Savoie and washed-rind Epoisses or Livarot; one fan loves it stirred into a homemade mayo and put on a burger; delicious on buttery toast or a grilled cheese with Brie and sliced apple. See Make It Your Own on pages 82–83 for unique flavor combinations and ingredients you can use to customize your own flavor.

I EAT NYC HOT PEPPER JELLY

| *Organic hot and sweet peppers float in organic apple cider vinegar with some sugar to balance the heat* |

I get my peppers from two places, the Brooklyn Grange farm in New York City and Z Food Farm in New Jersey. My boyfriend, Ben Flanner, is the founder and head farmer at the Grange and David Zabeck is the owner of Z Food Farm. Both of these farms are organic and run by young farmers who grow everything with love and extreme care. They have unique varieties of peppers, such as the Granada and my favorite this year, the ají dulce.

Experiment with whatever tasty peppers you can find, but remember that the more hot ones you add, the hotter your jelly will be. I like to balance the flavor with half hot peppers and half sweet peppers.

Spicy and sweet, you can put this jam on anything for an added punch of flavor; meat, cheese, and even omelets are enhanced—I love it on crackers with crème fraîche!

Makes About Five 8-ounce Jars

INGREDIENTS
1¾ pounds peppers, a mix of hot and sweet (to equal 6 cups sliced)
3 cups sugar (1½ pounds)
6 cups organic apple cider vinegar

FOR THE GELLING
See Chapter 3 for more information on pectin and calcium water
6 teaspoons calcium water
4 teaspoons pectin

SPECIAL EQUIPMENT
1 food processor

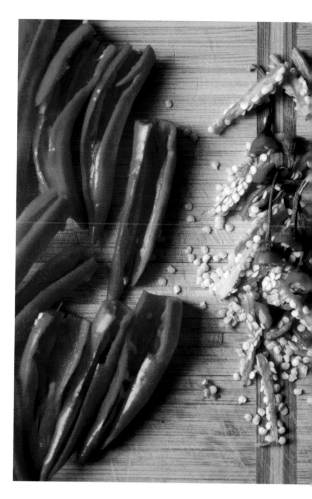

PREP

FOR THE PEPPERS:

Use gloves—these are hot peppers and they'll burn your skin! Slice the peppers open and remove the seeds. Place in a food processor and process until finely chopped. Alternately, you can finely dice the peppers by hand, but it will take a while.

Measure the peppers into a 6- to 8-quart nonreactive pot and add the proper amount of calcium water into the pan; stir well.

FOR THE JARS AND LIDS:

Wash and rinse the jars; put them into a big stockpot; cover the jars with water and bring to a boil; turn off the heat. Let stand in hot water until you are ready to fill.

Bring the lids and rings to a boil; turn off the heat. Let stand in hot water until you are ready to screw them onto the jars.

Place a few metal spoons in the freezer for testing the consistency and gel of your jam later. You can also place them in a cup of ice water, if you prefer.

For the sugar and pectin:

Measure the sugar into a separate bowl or measuring cup and thoroughly mix the proper amount of pectin powder into the sugar—using a fork helps to disperse the pectin into the sugar. Set the sugar mixture aside.

COOK

Add the vinegar to the peppers. Bring the fruit to a boil over medium-high heat. If it starts to foam, skim the foam off the top and discard the foam.

Pour the pectin-sugar mixture into the boiling jam slowly and carefully, stirring as you add. Stir vigorously for 1 to 2 minutes to dissolve the pectin.

Return the jam to a boil and remove from the heat. Skim off any and all foam that has formed on the top.

Pectin gels completely when thoroughly cool, so don't worry if your jam looks loose while still hot. To test, place a teaspoon of the hot jam onto one of the prepped frozen spoons; let it cool to room temperature (about 30 seconds) on the spoon. If it thickens up to the consistency desired, then the jam is ready. If not, mix in a little more pectin (½ teaspoon into ¼ cup sugar) and bring it to a boil again for 1 minute.

PRESERVE

See pages 29–30 for in-depth instructions on filling and processing the jars.

For this recipe, process the jars in a boiling water bath for 10 minutes.

TIPS

Pairs well with fresh ricotta cheese (see recipe on page 206) or with Valdeón and truffle salami; tastes great as a glaze or as an accompaniment to roast chicken or pork, and on grilled cheese with sharp Cheddar and sliced garlic (see recipe on page 213); delicious as a classic midwestern treat on Triscuits with cream cheese. See Make It Your Own on pages 82–83 for unique flavor combinations and ingredients you can use to customize your own flavor.

MAKE IT YOUR OWN

Once you've mastered the basic recipes, become daring and develop your own. Start with a basic recipe and then pick an herb, a spice, or an alcohol to add or substitute. The flavor chart below outlines my personal favorites, but feel free to create your own and go wild.

Rhubarb and Hibiscus Jam
Instead of hibiscus, substitute:
angelica (1 tablespoon, fresh)
bay leaf (3 leaves, fresh)
cloves (2 teaspoons, ground)
ginger (2 tablespoons, fresh)
kirsch (1 ounce)
spearmint (2 tablespoons, fresh)
nutmeg (2 teaspoons, ground)

Strawberry Balsamic Jam
Instead of vinegar, substitute:
brandy (1 ounce)
Champagne (1 cup)
Chartreuse (½ ounce)
Chianti (1 cup)
Pinot Noir (1 cup)

3's Company Triple-Berry Jam
Add 1 tablespoon each of one or more:
anise (2 teaspoons, ground)
brandy (1 ounce)
Cognac (1 ounce)
honey (2 ounces)
ginger (1 ounce)
kirsch (1 ounce)

Raspberry Rye Whiskey Jam
Instead of whiskey and mint, substitute:
Cognac (1 ounce) and cloves (2 teaspoons)
honey (2 ounces) and hazelnuts (¼ cup)
tequila (1 ounce) and sea salt (¼ teaspoon)
Riesling (I cup) and star anise (1 teaspoon, ground)
Champagne (1 cup) and lemon verbena (1 tablespoon)

Apricot Jam
Instead of thyme and vanilla, substitute:
saffron (¼ teaspoon) and honey (½ cup)
nutmeg (2 teaspoons) and orange liqueur (1 ounce)
pine nuts (¼ cup) and rosemary (8 sprigs)
almond extract (1 teaspoon) and Moscato d'Asti (1 cup)

Sugar Plum Fairy Jam
Instead of ice wine, substitute:
coriander (2 teaspoons) and port (1 ounce)
vanilla bean (1 bean) and whiskey (1 ounce)
nutmeg (2 teaspoons) and kirsch (1 ounce)
sage (2 tablespoons, fresh) and Shiraz wine (1 cup)

Really Rosie Jam
Instead of rose water, substitute:
Grand Marnier (1 tablespoon)
Himalayan salt (½ teaspoon)

mint, chocolate (½ cup)

orange zest and juice, from blood or Seville
orange (¼ cup)

pink peppercorns (1 teaspoon, ground)

white peaches (roughly 1 cup, chopped)

Thai Me Up Jam

Instead of Kaffir limes leaves, substitute:

honey (1 ounce)

peppercorns, Tellicherry (2 teaspoons, ground)

rose wine, sparkling (1 cup)

sea salt, gray (½ teaspoon)

Vin Santo wine (2 ounces)

Wild Blueberry Jam

Instead of rum, juniper, and anise,
substitute:

honey (1 ounce) and port (1 ounce)

lemon zest (½ teaspoon) and lemon thyme
(2 tablespoons, fresh)

cinnamon (1 teaspoon) and grade C maple
syrup (4 ounces)

Merlot (1 cup) and cloves (2 teaspoons)

Hot Fireman's Pear Jam

Instead of chipotle and cinnamon,
substitute:

ginger (2 tablespoons) and sea salt (½ teaspoon)

honey (1 ounce) and lime zest (½ teaspoon)

sage (2 tablespoons) and brandy (1 ounce)

orange blossom water (1 ounce) and cloves
(2 teaspoons)

sake (1 cup) and lemongrass (2 stems)

Figalicious Jam

Add 1 or 2 teaspoons of one or more:

anise, green (2 teaspoons, ground)

rosemary (8 sprigs, fresh)

port (1 ounce)

Pop's Sour Cherry Liqueur (page 185, 1 ounce)

cinnamon bark (2 teaspoons)

Watermelon and Lemongrass Jelly

Instead of lemongrass, substitute:

Sweet Cicely (1 tablespoon, fresh)

St. Germain (1 ounce)

angelica (1 tablespoon, fresh)

curry leaf (3 leaves, fresh)

Finger Lakes Wine Grape Jelly

Try another type of grape, such as
Merlot or Riesling, or add some spices for
a mulled-wine flavor, such as 1 teaspoon
ground cinnamon, ground cloves, and
orange zest.

Spiced Beer Jelly

Try adding 1 teaspoon ground cloves,
rosemary, thyme, or chamomile flowers.

I Eat NYC Hot Pepper Jelly

Instead of a mix of peppers, use a single
pepper, such as habanero, with a
tablespoon of mescal added.

Laena's Jam & Cheese Party
My Favorite Cheeses Paired with Preserved Fruit, Meat, Crackers, Toast, Nuts, and Fresh Veggies

CHEESES		BASE TEXTURE (crackers, toast, nuts)	PRESERVED FRUIT (jam, jelly, marmalade)	SAVORY (meat, veggies)	FRESH GREEN (herbs, greens)
BLOOMY BUTTERY CREAMY STINKY	Bonne Bouche, Camembert, Bucheron	almonds, rye toast	blueberry, blackberry, sour cherry	prosciutto, pork rillettes, pâté de campagne	radicchio
	Humboldt Fog	olive oil crackers	apricot, clementine	*finocchiona*, jamón serrano	basil, thyme
	Coupole, La Tur	toasted pistachios	pear, apple	duck rillettes	beets, beans
	Crottin	maple crackers, 7-grain toast	watermelon, plum	prosciutto, wild boar salami, grilled zucchini	mint, arugula
FRESH CREAMY SWEET TANGY	fresh mozzarella	olive oil grilled toast	fig, wine, garlic	pâté de foie gras, Calabrese salami	endive, hot peppers
	fresh ricotta *burrata*	sesame crackers	fig, hot pepper	smoked salmon, roasted eggplant, speck	radish, cucumber
	chèvre	oat crackers	spiced beer, strawberry, fig	wild mushrooms, truffle salami, spicy beef jerky	arugula
BLUE PUNCHY BITEY SPICY	Valdeón, Stilton, Gorgonzola	toasted walnuts	apple, strawberry	prosciutto, beef jerky	radish, endive, hot peppers
HARD DRY SNAPPY CARAMELLY	Mimolette, aged goat Gouda	fennel crackers	peach, nectarine, Meyer lemon	grilled beef, shiitake mushroom	pea shoots, dandelion
	Parmigiano-Reggiano, Vieille	olive oil crackers, toasted pecans	pear, plum, apricot	sage salami	arugula, hot peppers
FIRM LIMBER GRASSY	Drunken Goat, Malvarosa	sourdough toast	blood orange	Barolo salami	parsley
	sharp Cheddar	oat crackers, smoked almonds	pear, quince	pickled beets, speck	endive, arugula

5

PRESERVES, MARMALADE, AND CHUTNEY

Traveling and tasting my way around the world when I was in my twenties opened my eyes to the world of chutney, preserves, and marmalade. In New Zealand and Australia, I discovered preserves: whole perfect fruits suspended in their juices, with a looser consistency than the jam I grew up with in the United States. In India, I discovered chutney: sweet, savory, spicy, and prepared a million different ways. In Europe, I discovered marmalade: the perfect meld of bitter and sweet, presented in a translucent golden glow with big hunks of peel. As a kid, I hated marmalade—too bitter, I guess, for my palate; now I crave its bitter, sour, and lively flavor to wake up my senses.

The recipes in this chapter are all about intense and unique flavors. I often dub these "adult recipes" because they tend to be more appealing to a mature palate—from the tart, sweet, and downright beautiful Blood Orange Marmalade to the ode-to-late-fall Tipsy-Quince and Cranberry Chutney.

Most of the recipes can be made in the less-bountiful seasons of fall and winter with ingredients like plums, apples, and cranberries, as well as citrus and tropical fruits.

The recipes are followed by an extensive list on pages 128–129 of unique flavor combinations and ingredients you can use to customize your own preserves, chutneys, and marmalades.

Tiny Strawberry Preserves

Peachy Keen Preserves

Easy Like Sunday Morning Blueberry Preserves

Sour Cherry Preserves

Damson Plum Preserves

Purist Kumquat Marmalade

Grapefruit and Smoked Salt Marmalade

Blood Orange Marmalade

Clementine Marmalade

Meyer Lemon Marmalade

Brooklyn Green Tomato Chutney

Tipsy Quince and Cranberry Chutney

Mango and Lime Chutney

A NOTE ON CONSERVES AND PRESERVES

The term *conserve* is often used interchangeably with *preserve* in the United States, although traditionally *conserve* is used more specifically when nuts or dried fruits are added. For our purposes, we'll use *preserves* to mean whole fruit jams, made of fruit stewed in sugar and their own released juices.

Preserves often require an overnight maceration; that is, a steep in the fridge before you cook them to allow the sugar to penetrate the fruit, releasing the juices and heightening the flavor.

TINY STRAWBERRY PRESERVES

| *With Thai basil—small perfect strawberries pump up the volume of deliciousness* |

Small strawberries such as Mara des Bois or Earliglow are best to use for this recipe. Strawberries are easy to grow yourself, either in your backyard or on your fire escape. You can also find small strawberries at most farmers' markets; Norwich Meadows Farm sells them at the Union Square farmers' market in late May and June in New York City. Small, tart, and supersweet, these little strawberries are one of the best things about early summertime. Thai basil is milder than regular basil and has a slight anise flavor that works well with the strawberries.

This recipe is a two-day process, but the first day requires only about ten minutes of preparation.

Makes About Four 8-Ounce Jars or Two Pint Jars

INGREDIENTS
2¾ pounds fresh strawberries (about 6 cups)
2 cups sugar (1 pound)
2 tablespoons lemon juice
2 tablespoons Thai basil, leaves separated and stems discarded (about 2 ounces or
   1 small bunch)

SPECIAL EQUIPMENT
1 chinois sieve
1 candy thermometer

PREP
FOR THE STRAWBERRIES:
Rinse the berries and remove their hulls (green stems and leaves). Measure the fruit into a glass bowl or plastic food-safe Tupperware container and add the sugar and lemon juice.

Stir well. Refrigerate or leave in a cool place overnight or up to 24 hours so that the sugar and lemon juice are allowed to release the juice of the strawberries. Stir every so often to dissolve the sugar.

The next day, bring the macerated berry mixture to a simmer over medium-high heat to dissolve all the sugar; turn off the heat immediately and allow to macerate

1 more hour at room temperature. After 1 hour, stir gently and pour this mixture through a sieve. Place the collected syrup in a 6- to 8-quart nonreactive pot. Reserve the berries.

FOR THE JARS AND LIDS:

Wash and rinse the jars; put them into a big stockpot; cover the jars with water and bring to a boil; turn off the heat. Let stand in hot water until you are ready to fill.

Bring the lids and rings to a boil; turn off the heat. Let stand in hot water until you are ready to screw them onto the jars.

Place a few metal spoons in the freezer for testing the consistency and gel of your jam later. You can also place them in a cup of ice water, if you prefer.

COOK

Bring the collected syrup to a boil over high heat. Skim and continue cooking on high heat, stirring frequently to prevent scorching. The syrup will reach the gel stage at 221°F (105°C) on a candy thermometer, about 10 minutes. If you don't have a thermometer, test the consistency by placing a teaspoon of the hot syrup onto one of the prepped frozen spoons. Let it rest for a few minutes, then test the gel by tilting the spoon vertically; what is the consistency? If it runs loosely, then it's not done yet, but if it glides slowly along in a gloopy glob, then it's ready. If syrupy, bring it to a boil again for 1 to 5 minutes.

Add the reserved strawberries and the Thai basil. Return to a boil over high heat. Skim any foam that surfaces and bring back to a boil for 5 minutes, stirring gently to prevent scorching. Check the set with a cold spoon, as you did with the syrup. It should be firm and glide slowly down the spoon, and the strawberries should appear translucent.

Once it is done, turn off the heat.

PRESERVE

See pages 29–30 for in-depth instructions on filling and processing the jars.

For this recipe, process the jars in a boiling water bath for 6 minutes.

TIPS

Pairs well with fresh cheeses such as fresh ricotta (recipe on page 206), also good with punchy blue cheeses such as Valdeón and Stilton; great on a sandwich with grilled wild mushrooms and arugula; delicious on top of ice cream or yogurt. See Make It Your Own on pages 128–129 for unique flavor combinations and ingredients you can use to customize your own flavor.

PEACHY KEEN PRESERVES

| *With lemon verbena and cardamom—ripe summer peaches pop with fresh and lively flavors* |

There's something about a peach that evokes the essence of summer. As you take a bite of a fresh peach still warm from the sun and the juice drips down your chin, the sweet and spicy fruit tingles on your tongue in the most delightful way.

This recipe calls for fresh lemon verbena and ground green cardamom to bring out the flavor of the peaches even more. Lemon verbena *(Aloysia triphylla)* is native to South America, where it grows abundantly. The Spanish brought it to Europe in the 1700s, where it was used in perfume. It's usually difficult to find at grocery stores but is often sold at farmers' markets in the summer. Lemon verbena is easy to grow in an herb garden or in planters; the leaves can be used in tea and jam, and because they hold their scent and flavor well, they can be added to soaps, infused in oils, and used as potpourri.

This recipe is a two-day process, but the first day requires only about twenty minutes of preparation and cooking.

Makes About Four 8-Ounce Jars or Two Pint Jars

INGREDIENTS
2 pounds peaches (about 5 cups)
3 cups sugar (1½ pounds)
2 tablespoons lemon juice
½ teaspoon ground green cardamom
4 lemon verbena leaves

SPECIAL EQUIPMENT
1 piece cheesecloth
1 candy thermometer

PREP
FOR THE PEACHES:
Blanch the peaches in a pot of boiling water for about 1 minute. Refresh them by plunging in an ice water bath and leaving them there for at least 30 seconds; this will help loosen the peel and you should be able to easily pull it off with your hands. Halve the peaches and remove their pits, then cut each half into 6 slices.

Measure the fruit into a 6- to 8-quart nonreactive pot and add the sugar, lemon juice, cardamom, and the lemon verbena leaves tied in cheesecloth. Stir well.

Bring the fruit to a simmer over medium-high heat until bubbles appear around the edges. Turn off the heat and pour this mixture into a glass bowl or heat-safe Tupperware container and cover with parchment paper or a lid. Refrigerate for at least 6 hours or overnight.

FOR THE JARS AND LIDS:

Wash and rinse the jars; put them into a big stockpot; cover the jars with water and bring to a boil; turn off the heat. Let stand in hot water until you are ready to fill.

Bring the lids and rings to a boil; turn off the heat. Let stand in hot water until you are ready to screw them onto the jars.

Place a few metal spoons in the freezer for testing the consistency and gel of your jam later. You can also place them in a cup of ice water, if you prefer.

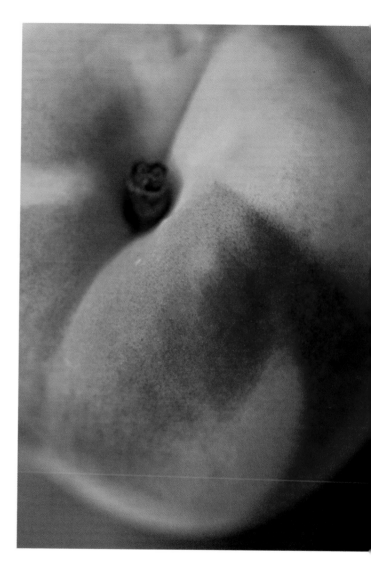

COOK

The next day, bring the fruit mixture to a boil over medium-high heat. If it starts to foam, skim the foam off the top and discard the foam. Remove the lemon verbena leaves in cheesecloth. Skim and continue cooking on high heat for 5 minutes, stirring gently and continuously to prevent scorching. Skim and return to a boil. The preserves will reach the gel stage at 221°F (105°C) on a candy thermometer, about 5 more minutes. If you don't have a thermometer, test the consistency by placing a teaspoon of the hot preserves onto one of the prepped frozen spoons. Let it rest for a few minutes, then test the gel by tilting the spoon vertically; what is the consistency? If the preserves run loosely like syrup, then it's not done yet, but if it glides slowly along in a gloopy glob, then it is ready. If syrupy, bring it to a boil again for 1 to 5 minutes.

PRESERVE

See pages 29–30 for in-depth instructions on filling and processing the jars.

For this recipe, process the jars in a boiling water bath for 6 minutes.

TIPS

Pairs well with hard cheeses such as Mimolette and aged Gouda; great on a sandwich with grilled beef and bitter dandelion greens; delicious on sourdough toast. See Make It Your Own on pages 128–129 for unique flavor combinations and ingredients you can use to customize your own flavor.

EASY LIKE SUNDAY MORNING
BLUEBERRY PRESERVES

| *With wild Maine blueberries and maple syrup—add this to your pancakes and swoon* |

When the wild blueberries of Maine are at their peak in August, we get our farmer friends to pick and freeze them so we can make our signature Easy Like Sunday Morning Blueberry Preserves all year long. Small, glossy, and more rich in flavor than their cultivated cousins, wild blueberries deliver a potent antioxidant punch—in fact, they have the highest antioxidant capacity per serving, compared with most other fruits. Adding a little maple syrup tastes just like Sunday morning should. I recommend using grade B syrup if you can find it, as it's a darker grade than the light A and has a rich, caramel flavor.

You can find frozen wild blueberries in most grocery stores, or you can pick your own in summer. Using frozen fruit is better than buying out-of-season fruit at the grocery store, because freezing preserves the perfect peak ripe flavor.

This recipe is a two-day process, but the first day requires only about twenty minutes of preparation and cooking. The next day, it should take less than an hour to complete the cooking and processing.

Makes About Four 8-Ounce Jars or Two Pint Jars

INGREDIENTS
2¼ pounds wild blueberries (about 6 cups)
3½ cups sugar (1¾ pounds)
2 ounces maple syrup
2 tablespoons lemon juice

Special Equipment
1 candy thermometer

PREP
For the blueberries:
Rinse the blueberries and remove their stems. Measure the fruit into a glass bowl or plastic heat-safe Tupperware container and add the sugar, maple syrup, and lemon juice. Macerate for 1 hour to let the juices release. Measure the fruit into a 6- to 8-quart nonreactive pot and bring it to a simmer over high heat. Once it simmers

and bubbles begin to appear at the sides, turn off the heat, pour it into the glass bowl or heat-safe plastic Tupperware container and cover with a lid or parchment paper. Refrigerate overnight or for up to 48 hours so that the sugar and lemon juice are allowed to release the juice of the blueberries.

FOR THE JARS AND LIDS:
Wash and rinse the jars; put them into a big stockpot; cover the jars with water and bring to a boil; turn off the heat. Let stand in hot water until you are ready to fill.

Bring the lids and rings to a boil; turn off the heat. Let stand in hot water until you are ready to screw them onto the jars.

Place a few metal spoons in the freezer for testing the consistency and gel of your jam later. You can also place them in a cup of ice water, if you prefer.

COOK

Once the juice is released, measure the fruit mixture into a 6- to 8-quart nonreactive pot and bring to a boil over medium-high heat. If it starts to foam, skim the foam off the top and discard the foam. Return to a boil and continue cooking on high heat for 5 minutes, stirring gently to prevent scorching.

Skim and return to a boil. The syrup will reach the gel stage at 221°F (105°C) on a candy thermometer, about 5 more minutes. If you don't have a thermometer, test the consistency by placing a teaspoon of the hot preserves onto one of the prepped frozen spoons. Let it rest for a few minutes, then test the gel by tilting the spoon vertically; what is the consistency? If the preserves run loosely like syrup, then it's not done yet, but if it glides slowly along in a gloopy glob, then the jam is ready. If syrupy, bring it to a boil again for 1 to 5 minutes.

PRESERVE

See pages 29–30 for in-depth instructions on filling and processing the jars.

For this recipe, process the jars in a boiling water bath for 6 minutes.

TIPS

Pairs well with soft cheeses such as Cambozola, Morbier, and Humboldt Fog; great on hearty wheat bread with a nice crispy crust and jamón serrano; delicious on top of ice cream or yogurt. See Make It Your Own on pages 128–129 for unique flavor combinations and ingredients you can use to customize your own flavor.

SOUR CHERRY PRESERVES

| *Sour cherries float in a red glow with hints of amaretto liqueur to enhance their flavor* |

Cherries are beloved in cultures all over the world and are preserved from Eastern Europe to Iran. Sour cherries in particular are rich in healthy antioxidants as well as high in vitamins, minerals, and phytochemicals. They're also one of the few foods to contain natural melatonin, which is a mood enhancer and sleep aid. Montmorency sour cherries are my favorite and have a slight almond flavor that's wonderful in these preserves.

To remove the pits, the best tool is a *snocciolatore* (pronounced *snoch-ol-atory*), or cherry pitter. It will make the job much easier. If you don't want to purchase a cherry pitter, then make a homemade version with a straw and an empty soda or beer bottle; set the cherry on the lip of the bottle and shove the straw into the center while

maintaining your grip on the cherry—the pit will fall into the jar.

This recipe uses added citrus pectin to minimize cooking time and to create a good set. You may prefer to omit the pectin and cook the jam for longer, until it congeals. This will give you a jam with a more caramelized flavor, but the cherries will also lose their structure.

Makes About Four 8-Ounce Jars or Two Pint Jars

INGREDIENTS

2 pounds sour cherries (about 5 cups)
3 tablespoons lemon juice
2¾ cups sugar (about 1¼ pounds)
¼ cup amaretto liqueur

For the Gelling

See Chapter 3 for more information on pectin and calcium water
3 teaspoons calcium water
2½ teaspoons pectin

SPECIAL EQUIPMENT
1 cherry pitter (snocciolatore), *or straw and bottle*

PREP

FOR THE CHERRIES:

Rinse the cherries and remove the stems. Using a cherry pitter or *snocciolatore*, remove all the pits from the cherries. Cut the cherries in halves.

Place the cherries and lemon juice in a 6- to 8-quart nonreactive pot and add the proper amount of calcium water into the pan; stir well.

FOR THE JARS AND LIDS:

Wash and rinse the jars; put them into a big stockpot; cover the jars with water and bring to a boil; turn off the heat. Let stand in hot water until you are ready to fill.

Bring the lids and rings to a boil; turn off the heat. Let stand in hot water until you are ready to screw them onto the jars.

Place a few metal spoons in the freezer for testing the consistency and gel of your jam later. You can also place them in a cup of ice water, if you prefer.

FOR THE SUGAR AND PECTIN:

Measure the sugar into a separate bowl or measuring cup and thoroughly mix the proper amount of pectin powder into the sugar—using a fork helps to disperse the pectin into the sugar. Set the sugar mixture aside.

COOK

Bring the cherries to a boil over high heat and continue cooking on high heat for 5 minutes. Skim and continue cooking on high heat, stirring frequently to prevent scorching. Add amaretto liqueur and return to a boil.

Pour the pectin-sugar mixture into the boiling jam slowly and carefully, stirring as you add. Stir vigorously for 1 to 2 minutes to dissolve the pectin.

Return to a boil and remove from the heat. Skim off any and all foam that has formed on the top.

Pectin gels completely when thoroughly cool, so don't worry if your jam looks loose when still hot. To test, place a teaspoon of the hot jam onto one of the prepped frozen spoons; let it cool to room temperature (about 30 seconds) on the spoon. If it thickens up to the consistency desired, then the jam is ready. If not, mix in a little more pectin (½ teaspoon into ¼ cup sugar) and bring it to a boil again for 1 minute.

PRESERVE

See pages 29–30 for in-depth instructions on filling and processing the jars.

For this recipe, process the jars in a boiling water bath for 6 minutes.

TIPS

Pairs well with soft cheese such as Bonne Bouche, Camembert, and Bucheron; great on pizza with barbecued pork and Manchego cheese; delicious on top of yogurt or ice cream. See Make It Your Own on pages 128–129 for unique flavor combinations and ingredients you can use to customize your own flavor.

DAMSON PLUM PRESERVES

| *Dark late-summer plums are given a rich and spicy flavor boost with port and ginger* |

Damson plums are easy to find at farmers' markets and special grocery stores in late summer throughout the northeast and northwest. They are oval and dark purple, almost black. They're delicate and should be used when they are slightly firm and just ripe.

In this recipe, port wine adds a sweet and rich flavor. Port wine is a fortified wine from Portugal, although the term is used in the United States for wines from anywhere that are made in the traditional manner. I've had great ports made in California! Traditionally, port is made from grapes grown in the Douro region of Portugal and is fortified by the addition of grape spirits that stop the fermentation and leave residual sugar in the wine, also boosting the alcohol content. It's often aged in caves before it is ready for drinking.

You can increase the ratio of alcohol in this recipe with a tablespoon more of port, if you fancy a boozier preserve. This recipe has little sugar, and with the addition of the skins, it is tart. If you like a sweeter preserve, test the flavor while cooking and add another ½ cup sugar to adjust.

This recipe is a two-day process, but the first day requires only about ten minutes of preparation. The next day, it should take less than an hour to complete the cooking and processing.

Makes About Four 8-Ounce Jars or Two Pint Jars

INGREDIENTS
2 pounds plums (about 6 cups)
2 cups sugar (1 pound)
3 tablespoons lemon juice
2 tablespoons minced fresh ginger
2 ounces port

PREP
FOR THE PLUMS:
Rinse the plums and halve them, leaving the skin on and discarding the pits. Measure the fruit into a glass bowl or plastic food-safe Tupperware container and add the sugar, lemon juice, and ginger.

Stir well. Macerate at room temperature for 1 hour, stir to help dissolve the sugar, then refrigerate or leave in a cool place overnight or up to 24 hours so that the sugar and lemon juice are allowed to release the juice of the plums.

The next day, place the plums and all their juice in a 6- to 8-quart nonreactive pot.

FOR THE JARS AND LIDS:

Wash and rinse the jars; put them into a big stockpot; cover the jars with water and bring to a boil; turn off the heat. Let stand in hot water until you are ready to fill.

Bring the lids and rings to a boil; turn off the heat. Let stand in hot water until you are ready to screw them onto the jars.

Place a few metal spoons in the freezer for testing the consistency and gel of your jam later. You can also place them in a cup of ice water, if you prefer.

COOK

Bring the plums to a boil over high heat and continue cooking on high heat for 5 minutes. Skim and continue cooking, stirring frequently to prevent scorching.

Add the port and return to a boil for another 5 minutes. Skim and return to a boil. The syrup will reach the gel stage at 221°F (105°C) on a candy thermometer, about 10 more minutes. If you don't have a thermometer, test the consistency by placing a teaspoon of the hot preserves onto one of the prepped frozen spoons. Let it rest for a few minutes, then test the gel by tilting the spoon vertically; what is the consistency? If the preserves run loosely like syrup then it's not done yet, but if it glides slowly along in a gloopy glob, then the preserves are ready. If syrupy, bring it to a boil again for 1 to 5 minutes.

Once done, give a last skim if there's any foam and turn off the heat.

PRESERVE

See pages 29–30 for in-depth instructions on filling and processing the jars.

For this recipe, process the jars in a boiling water bath for 6 minutes.

TIPS

Pairs well with bloomy cheese like Crottin or hard cheese such as Vieille; great on vegetable or pork dumplings; delicious on top of ice cream or yogurt and stirred into whipped cream to make the dessert plum fool. See Make It Your Own on pages 128–129 for unique flavor combinations and ingredients you can use to customize your own flavor.

PURIST KUMQUAT MARMALADE

| *Little oval kumquats dance to a beat all their own in this pure and simple marmalade* |

Kumquats are the most delightful little citrus fruits and are perfect all on their own: no pectin, no add-ins, no fancy booze, just kumquats and sugar.

Kumquats originated in Asia and were cultivated in China in the twelfth century; the word comes from the Cantonese *gam gwat*. They are much hardier fruits than oranges and can be grown in diverse climates. Unlike many oranges, the rind is sweet and the pulp is sour. They're great eaten raw but are also incorporated into many other dishes. In Corfu, Greece, they're made into a liqueur called Koum Quat, and in China they're often mixed with salt and buried inside a glass jar. Over time the salt releases the fruit's juices and they become tiny salty and sour kumquat pickles (see a similar recipe, Moroccan Preserved Lemons, in the "Pickled Fruit, Syrups, and Shrubs" chapter).

This recipe uses them to make a simple and delicious marmalade.

Makes About Four 8-Ounce Jars or Two Pint Jars

INGREDIENTS
2 pounds kumquats (about 6 cups)
3½ cups sugar (1¾ pounds)
2 tablespoons lemon juice
5 oranges, juiced to produce 1 cup (8 ounces)

Special Equipment
1 piece cheesecloth
1 candy thermometer

PREP
For the kumquats:
Kumquats have a hard peel and are small in size, so using a sharp paring knife to clean them will make life much easier. Take a slice off the end of each kumquat and then slice the fruit in half lengthwise. Pull out the central membrane that runs down the core of the fruit and pick the seeds out with the tip of the knife or with your fingers. Reserve the membrane and seeds in a small bowl, as they contain lots of pectin and will come in handy later when cooking the marmalade. Slice each kumquat half crosswise very thinly to make half moon–shaped pieces.

Toss the fruit and sugar, and lemon juice in a large glass, ceramic, or plastic container and mix gently to combine. Cover and let stand overnight or for at least 6 hours. Stir it halfway through.

Tie the seeds and inner membrane in a cheesecloth and place in a saucepan with the orange juice. Bring this mixture to a boil over medium-high heat, then reduce the heat to low, cover, and simmer for half an hour. Remove from the heat and let cool while you finish prepping.

When the cheesecloth bundle is cool enough to touch, gently squeeze it out over the pot to remove most of the liquid, squeezing and scraping off the gloopy liquid as it comes out into the water; the gloopy liquid is the natural pectin that's concentrated in the seeds and membrane! Give a stir to combine and set aside.

Place the kumquats and all their juices in a 6- to 8-quart nonreactive pot; add all the pectin-orange liquid and the cheesecloth with the seeds and membrane.

For the jars and lids:

Wash and rinse the jars; put them into a big stockpot; cover the jars with water and bring to a boil; turn off the heat. Let stand in hot water until you are ready to fill.

Bring the lids and rings to a boil; turn off the heat. Let stand in hot water until you are ready to screw them onto the jars.

Place a few metal spoons in the freezer for testing the consistency and gel of your jam later. You can also place them in a cup of ice water, if you prefer.

COOK

Bring the kumquat mixture to a boil over high heat and boil rapidly, stirring gently. Skim any foam that rises. Cook on high heat for 5 minutes. Skim again if necessary. Remove the cheesecloth with the seeds and membranes and stir again; return to a boil and boil rapidly for 10 minutes, stirring frequently.

The marmalade will reach the gel stage at 221°F (105°C) on a candy thermometer, about 20 more minutes. If you don't have a thermometer, test the consistency by placing a teaspoon of the hot marmalade onto one of the prepped frozen spoons. Let it rest for a few minutes, then test the gel by tilting the spoon vertically; what is the consistency? If the preserves run loosely like syrup then it's not done yet, but if it glides slowly along in a gloopy glob, then the marmalade is ready. If it is syrupy, bring it to a boil again for 1 to 5 minutes.

PRESERVE

See pages 29–30 for in-depth instructions on filling and processing the jars.

For this recipe, process the jars in a boiling water bath for 6 minutes.

TIPS

Pairs well with creamy, soft, and nutty cheeses such as Coulommiers and Tomme de Savoie; great on buttered whole-wheat toast with a poached or sunny-side-up egg; delicious with chocolate cookies. See Make It Your Own on pages 128–129 for unique flavor combinations and ingredients you can use to customize your own flavor.

GRAPEFRUIT AND SMOKED SALT MARMALADE

| *American-style marmalade, less bitter with a smooth jellied texture* |

Salt in marmalade? Yes, please. Salt gets a bad rap, and although in abundance it can be unhealthy, as a balanced ingredient salt helps enhance the flavor of foods. In this recipe, there's just a little salt, and it tames the bitterness and brightens the grapefruit flavor. This is one of our most popular flavors at stores and markets. Americans tend to be wary of marmalade's bitter flavor, so this mild marmalade appeals to most palates. Marmalades always contain the peel of the fruit, which gives the preserves their bitter flavor. This recipe uses just the zest and therefore is less bitter. It also has a smoother, almost jellylike texture.

Smoked salt is sea salt that's been smoked with wood such as alder, so that it becomes infused with the flavor of the wood. My favorite brand is Maldon smoked salt; it's gently smoky and the salt crystals are thin and deliciously briny, melting nicely into the jam.

The style of this marmalade is unusual and the method of preparation is modern, therefore traditionalists may balk (pectin? straining the juice?), but trust me, this stuff is so good that the traditionalists will be converted. If your grandma disapproves, just tell her to wait and taste the final product. Serve it on a nice scone or piece of toast and everyone will be happy.

Also try this marmalade in cocktails; my jam apprentice, Emma, loves to stir it into gin with a splash of soda water. Jam on!

Makes About Six 8-Ounce Jars or Three Pint Jars

INGREDIENTS
12 medium grapefruits (to equal 6 cups juice)
2 tablespoons lemon juice
3 cups sugar (1½ pounds)
smoked salt

For the Gelling
See Chapter 3 for more information on pectin and calcium water
4 teaspoons calcium water
3 teaspoons pectin

PREP

FOR THE GRAPEFRUIT:

Zest 6 of the grapefruits and reserve. Slice the grapefruits in half and juice them in a juicer or with your hands; strain the juice to remove any seeds.

Measure the juice and all the zest into a 6- to 8-quart nonreactive pot and add lemon juice and the proper amount of calcium water into the pan; stir well.

FOR THE JARS AND LIDS:

Wash and rinse the jars; put them into a big stockpot; cover the jars with water and bring to a boil; turn off the heat. Let stand in hot water until you are ready to fill.

Bring the lids and rings to a boil; turn off the heat. Let stand in hot water until you are ready to screw them onto the jars.

Place a few metal spoons in the freezer for testing the consistency and gel of your jam later. You can also place them in a cup of ice water, if you prefer.

FOR THE SUGAR AND PECTIN:
Measure the sugar into a separate bowl or measuring cup, add the smoked salt, and thoroughly mix the proper amount of pectin powder into the sugar—using a fork helps to disperse the pectin into the sugar. Set the sugar-salt mixture aside.

COOK

Bring the fruit juice and zest to a boil over medium-high heat. If it starts to foam, skim the foam off the top and discard the foam. Be watchful; this marmalade has a tendency to foam over. If this starts to happen, reduce the heat to low until it calms down, then return to a boil.

Pour the pectin-sugar mixture into the boiling jam slowly and carefully, stirring as you add. Stir vigorously for 1 to 2 minutes to dissolve the pectin.

Return the fruit to a boil and remove from the heat. Skim off any and all foam that has formed on the top.

Pectin gels completely when thoroughly cool, so don't worry if your jam looks loose while still hot. To test, place a teaspoon of the hot jam onto one of the prepped frozen spoons; let it cool to room temperature (about 30 seconds) on the spoon. If it thickens up to the consistency desired, then the jam is ready. If not, mix in a little more pectin (½ teaspoon into ¼ cup sugar) and bring it to a boil again for 1 minute.

PRESERVE

See pages 29–30 for in-depth instructions on filling and processing the jars.

For this recipe, process the jars in a boiling water bath for 6 minutes.

TIPS

Pairs well with creamy cheese such as *mozzarella di bufala* and *burrata;* tastes great as a glaze on fish or with poached eggs and toast (recipe on page 201); delicious stirred into gin cocktails, such as a grapefruit gin fizz with St. Germain elderflower liqueur and a splash of tonic. See Make It Your Own on pages 128–129 for unique flavor combinations and ingredients you can use to customize your own flavor.

BLOOD ORANGE MARMALADE

| *With brandy—beautiful blood orange peel floats in golden red jelly,*
gorgeous on the breakfast table |

Blood Orange Marmalade is the perfect antidote to the doldrums of winter, or if you live in warmer climates, then it's an antidote to a dreary rainy week. I like the Moro variety, which are the most colorful of the blood oranges, with a deep red flesh and a rind that has a bright red blush. The flavor is strong and the aroma is intense, bitter, and has a hint of tart raspberry. Blood oranges are nutritious—their red pigment (officially, *anthocyanin*) is an antioxidant that may diminish the risk of heart disease, some types of cancer, cholesterol accumulation, and cataracts, plus they're chock-full of vitamin C and that great citrus taste that I crave in cold or dreary weather. With the addition of a little brandy, this marmalade is both delicious and cozy.

Makes About Six 8-Ounce Jars or Three Pint Jars

INGREDIENTS

1½ pounds green apples, such as Granny Smith
4 pounds blood oranges (about 12; to equal 4 cups juice)
4 cups sugar (about 2 pounds)
2 tablespoons lemon juice
2 ounces brandy

Special Equipment
1 square cheesecloth
1 chinois sieve or jelly bag
1 candy thermometer

PREP

For the apples:

Rinse the apples and remove their stems. Cut the apples into quarters without peeling or coring them.

Place the apples in a 6- to 8-quart nonreactive pot and cover them with water. Bring to a boil and allow them to simmer for 30 minutes on low heat until the apples are soft.

Collect the juice made by the apples by pouring them through a sieve or jelly bag, pressing lightly on the fruit to release the juice. Allow the juice to drain completely, preferably overnight in the refrigerator, so you have the proper 2½ cups.

FOR THE BLOOD ORANGES:

The next day, slice the blood oranges in half and juice them in a juicer or with your hands; strain the juice and reserve any seeds as well as the skin of 2 oranges. Using a spoon, scrape the membrane, white pith, and any excess fibers out of the reserved orange skins; place the membrane and seeds in a piece of cheesecloth and tie shut. Using a sharp paring knife, slice the peel into ¼-inch thin strips.

Blanch the peel in 2 cups water by bringing the water to a boil, then discarding the water. Add new water, bring to a boil again, discard the water; repeat three more times.

Place the apple juice, orange juice, sugar, lemon juice, blood orange peel, brandy, and the seeds and membrane in cheesecloth into a 6- to 8-quart Dutch oven or a stainless-steel or copper pot.

FOR THE JARS AND LIDS:

Wash and rinse the jars; put them into a big stockpot; cover the jars with water and bring to a boil; turn off the heat. Let stand in hot water until you are ready to fill.

Bring the lids and rings to a boil; turn off the heat. Let stand in hot water until you are ready to screw them onto the jars.

Place a few metal spoons in the freezer for testing the consistency and gel of your jam later. You can also place them in a cup of ice water, if you prefer.

COOK

Bring the fruit to a boil over high heat and boil rapidly, stirring gently. Skim any foam that rises. Cook on high heat for 10 minutes, stirring constantly. Skim again if necessary. Remove the cheesecloth with the seeds and membrane and stir; return to a boil and boil rapidly for 10 minutes, stirring frequently.

The syrup will reach the gel stage at 221°F (105°C) on a candy thermometer, about 10 more minutes. If you don't have a thermometer, test the consistency by placing a teaspoon of the hot marmalade onto one of the prepped frozen spoons. Let it rest for a few minutes, then test the gel by tilting the spoon vertically; what is the consistency? If the marmalade runs loosely like syrup, then it's not done yet, but if it glides slowly along in a gloopy glob, then the marmalade is ready. If syrupy, bring it to a boil again for 1 to 5 minutes.

PRESERVE

See pages 29–30 for in-depth instructions on filling and processing the jars.

For this recipe, process the jars in a boiling water bath for 6 minutes.

TIPS

Pairs well with strong and creamy blue cheese such as a Fourme d'Ambert or a creamy and sweet Cantalet; great on buttered whole-wheat toast; delicious with chocolate or ginger cookies. See Make It Your Own on pages 128–129 for unique flavor combinations and ingredients you can use to customize your own flavor.

CLEMENTINE MARMALADE

| *A sweet and tart, slightly bitter, fun and flirty classic French marmalade* |

Clementine oranges are a harbinger of winter and the holiday season, and one of the addictive joys of the cold months. This marmalade preserves their fun color and sweet flavor.

My friend Gregory brought me a jar of clementine marmalade from Paris the year I began my business, and I was enchanted by the perfect circles of fruit suspended in a golden orange jelly—so beautiful and so tasty. I worked hard to create my own version of this classic, and I think you'll enjoy eating this for breakfast on a blustery winter day, with a hot cup of black tea steaming beside you.

This recipe uses pectin to shorten the cooking time and to preserve the shape and texture of the fruit. This recipe takes a few days to complete, but don't be intimidated. The first two days require just ten minutes each day to prep and macerate the fruit. The third day should take less than an hour to complete.

Makes About Four 8-Ounce Jars or Two Pint Jars

INGREDIENTS
1¾ pounds clementine oranges (about 6 cups sliced)
3 cups sugar (1½ pounds)
2 tablespoons lemon juice

FOR THE GELLING
See Chapter 3 for more information on pectin and calcium water
2 teaspoons pectin
3 teaspoons calcium water

PREP
FOR THE CLEMENTINES:
Use a sharp knife to take a slice off both ends of each clementine. Keeping the peels on, cut the clementines into very thin round slices; remove any seeds. Cut the round slices into quarters.

In a large glass, ceramic, or plastic container, combine the quartered clementine slices, 1 cup sugar, and the lemon juice. Cover and let stand overnight.

For the jars and lids:

Wash and rinse the jars; put them into a big stockpot; cover the jars with water and bring to a boil; turn off the heat. Let stand in hot water until you are ready to fill.

Bring the lids and rings to a boil; turn off the heat. Let stand in hot water until you are ready to screw them onto the jars.

Place a few metal spoons in the freezer for testing the consistency and gel of your jam later. You can also place them in a cup of ice water, if you prefer.

For the sugar and pectin:

Measure the remaining 2 cups sugar into a separate bowl or measuring cup and thoroughly mix the proper amount of pectin powder into the sugar—using a fork helps to disperse the pectin into the sugar. Set the sugar mixture aside.

COOK

The next day, place the fruit mixture in a 6- to 8-quart nonreactive pot. Bring to a simmer and turn off the heat. Return the fruit mixture to the glass, ceramic, or plastic container and let stand overnight.

The third day, return the fruit mixture to the 6- to 8-quart nonreactive pot and add the proper amount of calcium water into the pan; stir well.

Bring the fruit to a boil over medium-high heat. If it starts to foam, skim the foam off the top and discard the foam. Pour the pectin-sugar mixture into the boiling jam slowly and carefully, stirring as you add. Stir vigorously for 1 to 2 minutes to dissolve the pectin.

Return the fruit to a boil and remove from the heat. Skim off any and all foam that has formed on the top.

Pectin gels completely when thoroughly cool, so don't worry if your jam looks loose when still hot. To test, place a teaspoon of the hot jam onto one of the prepped frozen spoons; let it cool to room temperature (about 30 seconds) on the spoon. If it thickens up to the consistency desired, then the jam is ready. If not, mix in a little more pectin (½ teaspoon into ¼ cup sugar) and bring it to a boil again for 1 minute.

PRESERVE

See pages 29–30 for in-depth instructions on filling and processing the jars.

For this recipe, process the jars in a boiling water bath for 6 minutes.

TIPS

Pairs well with dense, peppery goat cheeses like Chabichou or Crottin de Chavignol; tastes great with chocolate tarts; delicious stirred into salad dressing for an endive salad with olives and anchovies. See Make It Your Own on pages 128–129 for unique flavor combinations and ingredients you can use to customize your own flavor.

MEYER LEMON MARMALADE

| *With bay leaf and absinthe—floral and herbaceous notes elevate this tasty marmalade* |

Meyer lemons are amazingly sweet and tart, with a uniquely perfumed flavor. It used to be difficult to find them outside of California, but over the last few years, they've begun to pop up in specialty fruit markets and grocery stores across the country.

I tasted Meyer lemons for the first time as a teenager while visiting California and I was hooked. I love to use this marmalade in diverse dishes, to brighten my toast, to glaze fish, or to mix into salad dressing. The bay leaf and absinthe complement the floral perfumed notes of the lemons, making this a perfect marmalade for dreary winter mornings.

Makes About Four 8-Ounce Jars or Two Pint Jars

INGREDIENTS

1½ pounds green apples, such as Granny Smith
8 bay leaves
5 pounds Meyer lemons (about 12; to equal 4 cups juice)
4 cups sugar (2 pounds)
1 ounce absinthe, such as Pacific Distillery Pacifique Absinthe Verte Supérieure or Vieux Carre

SPECIAL EQUIPMENT
1 piece cheesecloth
1 chinois sieve or jelly bag
1 candy thermometer

PREP

FOR THE APPLES:
Rinse the apples and remove their stems. Cut the apples into quarters without peeling or coring them. Bruise the bay leaves with the back of a knife or mallet.

Place the apples and the bay leaves in a 6- to 8-quart nonreactive pot and cover them with water. Bring to a boil over medium-high heat, reduce the heat, and allow them to simmer for 30 minutes on low heat until the apples are soft.

Collect the juice made by the apples by pouring them through a sieve or jelly bag, pressing lightly on the fruit to release the juice. Allow the juice to drain completely,

for at least 3 hours or preferably overnight in the refrigerator, so you have the proper 2½ cups.

FOR THE MEYER LEMONS:
The next day, slice the lemons in half and juice them in a juicer or by hand; strain the juice and reserve any seeds as well as the skin of 3 lemons. Using a spoon, scrape the membrane, white pith, and any excess fibers out of the reserved lemon skins; place the membrane and seeds in a piece of cheesecloth and tie shut. Using a sharp paring knife, slice the peel into ¼-inch thin strips.

Place the apple juice, lemon juice, lemon peel, sugar, and the seeds and membrane mixture in cheesecloth in a 6- to 8-quart nonreactive pot.

FOR THE JARS AND LIDS:
Wash and rinse the jars; put them into a big stockpot; cover the jars with water and bring to a boil; turn off the heat. Let stand in hot water until you are ready to fill.

Bring the lids and rings to a boil; turn off the heat. Let stand in hot water until you are ready to screw them onto the jars.

Place a few metal spoons in the freezer for testing the consistency and gel of your jam later. You can also place them in a cup of ice water, if you prefer.

COOK
Bring the fruit to a boil over high heat and boil rapidly, stirring gently. Skim any foam that rises. Cook on high heat for 10 minutes, stirring constantly. Skim again if necessary. Remove the cheesecloth with the seeds and membrane and stir; add the absinthe, return to a boil, and boil rapidly for 10 minutes, stirring frequently.

The syrup will reach the gel stage at 221°F (105°C) on a candy thermometer, about 10 more minutes. If you don't have a thermometer, test the consistency by placing a teaspoon of the hot marmalade onto one of the prepped frozen spoons. Let it rest for a few minutes, then test the gel by tilting the spoon vertically; what is the consistency? If the marmalade runs loosely like syrup then it's not done yet, but if it glides slowly along in a gloopy glob, then the marmalade is ready. If it is syrupy, bring it to a boil again for 1 to 5 minutes.

PRESERVE

See pages 29–30 for in-depth instructions on filling and processing the jars.

For this recipe, process the jars in a boiling water bath for 6 minutes.

TIPS

Pairs well with strong and creamy blue cheese such as a Fourmet d'Ambert or a washed-rind Gabietou or Meadow Creek Grayson; great on buttered multigrain toast and gingerbread; delicious stirred into salad dressing for a fresh crab salad or served alongside pork cutlets. See Make It Your Own on pages 128–129 for unique flavor combinations and ingredients you can use to customize your own flavor.

BROOKLYN GREEN TOMATO CHUTNEY

| *The last harvest green tomatoes with vinegar, spices, and vermouth, cooked down into chutney* |

Green tomatoes may conjure the first frost and the sad end to summer's vegetable bounty, but they're also a way to preserve the perfect tang of a fresh tomato. I like to make them into this chutney or pickle them with raw garlic cloves, tons of mustard seed, coriander, and apple cider vinegar.

To keep things interesting in the Anarchy kitchen, I add currants, chili peppers, sweet vermouth, onions, mustard seeds, smoked paprika, sugar, and organic cider vinegar to this chutney. It's kick ass and a worthy accompaniment to a number of meals. Smear it on roast chicken, nibble it with toast, swirl some in your polenta, or enjoy a dollop alongside some perfectly poached eggs, and you won't be sorry. This chutney delivers any time you want a tangy tomato accompaniment to a meal.

Makes About Four 8-Ounce Jars or Two Pint Jars

INGREDIENTS

2 pounds unripe tomatoes (about 2¾ cups, diced)
1 medium onion, diced (1 cup)
¼ cup currants
2 small hot chili peppers
½ cup sweet vermouth
3 tablespoons brown sugar
2 teaspoons mustard seeds
½ teaspoon chili pepper flakes
¼ teaspoon smoked paprika
½ cup water
3 tablespoons cider vinegar
½ teaspoon salt
¼ pound ripe tomatoes (about 1 cup, diced)

PREP

FOR THE TOMATOES, ONIONS, AND SPICES:
Measure the diced unripe tomatoes, diced onion, currants, chili peppers, sweet vermouth, brown sugar, mustard seeds, chili pepper flakes, smoked paprika, water, vinegar, and salt into a 6- to 8-quart nonreactive pot; stir well.

F OR THE JARS AND LIDS:

Wash and rinse the jars; put them into a big stockpot; cover the jars with water and bring to a boil; turn off the heat. Let stand in hot water until you are ready to fill.

Bring lids and rings to a boil; turn off the heat. Let stand in hot water until you are ready to screw them onto the jars.

Place a few metal spoons in the freezer for testing the consistency and gel of your jam later. You can also place them in a cup of ice water, if you prefer.

COOK

Bring the unripe tomato mixture to a boil over high heat, reduce the heat, and simmer for 25 minutes before adding the ripe tomatoes. Continue to simmer until the tomatoes are tender and the texture is thickened, about 1 hour. Give an occasional stir to prevent sticking, and stir more frequently as the cooking nears completion. Be careful, as the hot liquid can splatter as you stir! When the mixture is thickened and looks like chutney (as opposed to tomato sauce), it's done. It will produce a deeper sounding bubble and thicken as it nears completion.

To test, place a teaspoon of the hot chutney onto one of the prepped frozen spoons. Place it back in the freezer, with the chutney on it, for 3 to 4 minutes. Remove the spoon and test the gel by tilting the spoon vertically. What is the consistency? If it's thick, then it's ready. If liquid pools around the edges and it looks syrupy, bring it to a boil again for 5 minutes.

Once it is done, give it a quick stir and turn off the heat.

PRESERVE

See pages 29–30 for in-depth instructions on filling and processing the jars.

For this recipe, process the jars in a boiling water bath for 10 minutes.

TIPS

Pairs well with sweet, nutty cheeses like Gruyère or Ewephoria Sheep Milk Gouda; great with roast chicken or stirred into risotto; delicious with poached eggs and toast. See Make It Your Own on pages 128–129 for unique flavor combinations and ingredients you can use to customize your own flavor.

TIPSY QUINCE AND CRANBERRY CHUTNEY

| *Fragrant and quirky quince with whiskey-soaked raisins make a perfect holiday chutney* |

Quince is a beautiful fruit, laden with a fuzzy grayish "pubescence" and an intensely perfumed and hard flesh. Rarely seen in the average grocery store, the fruit is green when first picked and deepens in late autumn to yellow. The rareness of quince is not due to its fragileness or the climate it needs, since like apples, quince grow all over the world, from the Middle East where they originated to Northern Europe and throughout the United States. Quince is an ancient fruit, and history is laden with references. Quince was cultivated before apples, and many historical references mix up these similar fruits. The ancient Greeks offered quince at weddings because they were considered sacred to the goddess Aphrodite, and Plutarch claims that a Greek bride would take a bite of quince to perfume her kiss before entering the bridal chamber. In Greek mythology, Paris gave Aphrodite a quince and Atalanta paused in her famous race to pluck the golden fruit. The Roman cookbook *Apicius* supplies recipes for stewing quince with honey.

In my recipe, cranberries add a beautiful pink hue to the chutney, and whiskey-soaked raisins warm up the flavor. Use fresh cranberries if you can find them.

Choose ripe (yellow-colored), mostly unblemished quince. Quince can get gnarled and blemished as they ripen, and you will lose much of your yield if you use poor-quality fruit.

Makes About Four 8-Ounce Jars or Two Pint Jars

INGREDIENTS
2 tablespoons flame raisins
2 ounces whiskey
1 pound medium quince (about 3; to equal about 3 cups diced)
1 pound fresh, whole cranberries (about 4 cups)
1 cup sugar (½ pound)
1 cup apple cider vinegar
½ cup water

PREP
FOR THE QUINCE:
Place the raisins in a bowl and cover with the whiskey; soak them for 30 minutes or

more while you prep the quince. Rinse and peel the quince. Remove any rotten or blemished flesh, then core and dice. Rinse the cranberries and drain; set aside. Measure the quince, sugar, whiskey-soaked raisins (add the soaking whiskey, too), vinegar, and water into a 6- to 8-quart nonreactive pot; stir well.

FOR THE JARS AND LIDS:

Wash and rinse the jars; put them into a big stockpot; cover the jars with water and bring to a boil; turn off the heat. Let stand in hot water until you are ready to fill.

Bring the lids and rings to a boil; turn off the heat. Let stand in hot water until you are ready to screw them onto the jars.

Place a few metal spoons in the freezer for testing the consistency and gel of your jam later. You can also place them in a cup of ice water, if you prefer.

COOK

Bring the fruit mixture to a boil over high heat, stirring frequently to prevent scorching. Reduce the heat and cook uncovered at a steady simmer for 30 minutes.

Add the cranberries and cook for 30 more minutes. Gradually reduce the heat if the jam starts to stick and scorch. Keep a watchful eye and stir vigilantly for the last 5 to 10 minutes to prevent scorching. When the chutney has thickened and big bubbles are popping all over the surface, test for consistency.

To test, place a teaspoon of the hot chutney onto one of the prepped frozen spoons. Place it back in the freezer, with the chutney on it, for 3 to 4 minutes. Remove the spoon and test the gel by tilting the spoon vertically. What is the consistency? If it's thick, then it's ready. If liquid pools around the edges and it looks syrupy, bring it to a boil again for 5 minutes.

Once it is done, give it a quick stir and turn off the heat.

PRESERVE

See pages 29–30 for in-depth instructions on filling and processing the jars.

For this recipe, process the jars in a boiling water bath for 10 minutes.

TIPS

Pairs well with bold cheeses such as Cabra Romero or a luscious Brillat Savarin; great on a grilled cheese and ham sandwich; delicious with roast chicken and rice dishes. See Make It Your Own on pages 128–129 for unique flavor combinations and ingredients you can use to customize your own flavor.

MANGO AND LIME CHUTNEY

| *Southeast Asian–style chutney with Kaffir lime leaves and spices* |

Chutney is a spicy condiment made of fruits or vegetables with vinegar, spices, and sugar, originating in India. But growing up in the United States, I had only tasted chutney from the supermarket. Most of it was bland and very sweet. It wasn't until I traveled to India that I discovered the true nature of the south Asian condiment. And recently at an underground supper club in the Fort Greene neighborhood of Brooklyn where I was a guest chef, an Indian woman schooled me on chutney's true nature, even sharing her grandmother's recipe with me, which I've adapted here.

Called *chatni* in India, chutney is a spicy relish meant to accompany less-flavorful foods, such as rice or dal. It's usually prepared fresh as opposed to bought canned, and is made by combining spices and herbs such as ginger, chili pepper, mint, or coriander leaves for a spicy flavor with garlic, lime, tamarind, or coconut for a sour flavor, and then with fruit such as mango for a sweet flavor. The sour tang of this condiment is part of its appeal and makes it a versatile accompaniment to sandwiches, rice dishes, roast meat such as chicken, or any neutral-tasting food.

This recipe uses south Asian ingredients like mango, lime, and spices. There are two more obscure ingredients: *kecap manis*, an Indonesian and Malaysian sweet soy sauce, and Kaffir lime leaf. If you can't find fresh or frozen Kaffir lime leaves, simply omit them as there's no substitute. If you live in a medium to large city, you should be able to find *kecap manis* at Southeast Asian grocery stores. You can also find it online. It's delicious and has a unique flavor that's very different from tamari or regular soy sauce. I'm totally obsessed with it, and my favorite brand is Bango—I put it in everything from rice to salad dressing. If you can't find *kecap manis*, substitute with mild, fancy-grade molasses.

Makes About Six 8-Ounce Jars or Three Pint Jars

INGREDIENTS

2 limes (to equal ½ cup chopped)
1 orange (to equal ½ cup chopped)
6 small mangoes (to equal 4 cups chopped)
1 medium onion, coarsely chopped (1 cup)
1 cup lightly packed brown sugar

1 cup apple cider vinegar
¼ cup honey
2 fresh small red chilies, finely chopped, with seeds
2 cloves garlic, minced
½ cup minced fresh ginger
¼ cup kecap manis *(Indonesian sweet soy sauce)*
2 tablespoons finely chopped cilantro
1 tablespoon mustard seeds
1 tablespoon coriander seeds
1 teaspoon ground cloves
1 teaspoon ground cinnamon
4 fresh Kaffir lime leaves

PREP

FOR THE FRUIT AND SPICES:

Zest the limes and orange. Peel and chop them, removing the seeds and white pith. Chop the mango by making 4 lengthwise cuts to the pit. Cut away the quarters and chop the flesh. Combine the chopped mango, chopped onion, brown sugar, vinegar, honey, chopped limes, and orange, lime and orange zest, chilies, garlic, ginger, and *kecap manis* in a 6- to 8-quart nonreactive pot; stir well.

FOR THE JARS AND LIDS:

Wash and rinse the jars; put them into a big stockpot; cover the jars with water and bring to a boil; turn off the heat. Let stand in hot water until you are ready to fill.

Bring the lids and rings to a boil; turn off the heat. Let stand in hot water until you are ready to screw them onto the jars.

Place a few metal spoons in the freezer for testing the consistency and gel of your jam later. You can also place them in a cup of ice water, if you prefer.

COOK

Bring the fruit mixture to a boil over medium-high heat, stirring frequently to prevent scorching. Reduce the heat to low and cook uncovered at a steady simmer for 30 minutes, stirring frequently. Add the cilantro, mustard seeds, coriander seed, cloves, cinnamon, and Kaffir lime leaves. Gradually reduce the heat if the jam starts to stick and scorch. Keep a watchful eye and stir vigilantly for the last 5 to 10 minutes to prevent scorching. When the chutney has thickened and big bubbles are popping all over the surface, test for consistency.

To test, place a teaspoon of the hot chutney onto one of the prepped frozen spoons. Place it back in the freezer, with the chutney on it, for 3 to 4 minutes. Remove the spoon and test the gel by tilting the spoon vertically. What is the consistency? If it's thick, then it's ready. If liquid pools around the edges and it looks syrupy, bring it to a boil again for 5 minutes.

Once done, give it a quick stir and turn off the heat.

PRESERVE

See pages 29–30 for in-depth instructions on filling and processing the jars.

For this recipe, process the jars in a boiling water bath for 10 minutes.

TIPS

Pairs well with milky and sweet Asiago Pressato or creamy taleggio; great with roast meat and on turkey sandwiches; delicious served with rice and dal. See Make It Your Own on pages 128–129 for unique flavor combinations and ingredients you can use to customize your own flavor.

MAKE IT YOUR OWN

Once you've mastered the basic recipes, become daring and develop your own. Start with a basic recipe and then pick an herb, a spice, or an alcohol to add or substitute. The flavor chart below outlines my personal favorites, but feel free to create your own and go wild.

Tiny Strawberry Preserves
Add 1 tablespoon of herbs or spices:
basil (2 tablespoons, fresh)
bay leaf (5 leaves, fresh)
cardamom (2 teaspoons, ground)
chervil (1 tablespoon, fresh)
cinnamon (2 teaspoons, ground)
thyme (1 tablespoon, fresh)

Peachy Keen Preserves
Add 1 tablespoon of herbs or spices:
nutmeg (2 teaspoons, ground)
chervil (1 tablespoon, fresh)
cinnamon (2 teaspoons, ground)
thyme (1 tablespoon, fresh)

Easy Like Sunday Morning Blueberry Preserves
Instead of maple syrup, substitute:
brandy (1 ounce)
bourbon (1 ounce)
Ginger Syrup (1 ounce, page 190)

Sour Cherry Preserves
Add one or more of the following:
brandy (1 ounce)
balsamic vinegar (1 ounce)

jalapeño peppers (¼ cup, diced)
nutmeg (1 teaspoon)

Damson Plum Preserves
Instead of port and ginger, substitute:
*nutmeg (1 teaspoon) and orange liqueur
    (2 ounces)*
*cardamom (1 teaspoon) and Ginger Syrup
    (1 ounce, page 190)*
*rosemary (6 sprigs, fresh) and whiskey
    (2 ounces)*

Purist Kumquat Marmalade
Add one or more of the following:
sea salt (½ teaspoon)
fresh ginger (2 tablespoons)
Key lime zest and juice (¼ cup)
cloves (1 teaspoon, ground)
Grand Marnier (1 ounce)

Grapefruit and Smoked Salt Marmalade
Instead of smoked salt, substitute:
rosemary (1 tablespoon, fresh)
ginger (2 tablespoons, fresh)
jalapeño peppers (2 tablespoons, fresh)
gin (2 ounces)

Blood Orange Marmalade

Instead of brandy, substitute:

bourbon (2 ounces)

maple syrup (2 ounces)

chamomile flower syrup (1 ounce)

Clementine Marmalade

Add one or more of the following:

sea salt (½ teaspoon)

nutmeg (2 teaspoons, ground)

vanilla bean (1 bean)

Pop's Sour Cherry Liqueur (2 ounces,
page 185)

Meyer Lemon Marmalade

Instead of bay leaf and absinthe,
substitute:

ginger (2 tablespoons) and sea salt
(½ teaspoon)

whiskey (1 ounce) and cardamom
(1 teaspoon)

sage (2 tablespoons) and brandy
(1 ounce)

orange blossom water (1 ounce) and cloves
(2 teaspoons)

sake (1 cup) and lemongrass (2 stems)

Brooklyn Green Tomato Chutney

Add one or more of the following:

fresh ginger (2 tablespoons)

cardamom (1 teaspoon, ground)

Ginger Syrup (1 ounce, page 190)

Tipsy Quince and Cranberry Chutney

Try adding 1 teaspoon ground cloves or
rosemary; or 1 tablespoon pine nuts,
fresh ginger; or Pop's Sour Cherry
Liqueur (2 ounces, page 185).

Mango and Lime Chutney

Try adding 1 tablespoon coriander seeds,
fresh ginger, or Key lime juice and zest.

SUGAR-FREE JAM AND FRUIT BUTTER

If your diet doesn't allow for sugar or you just don't like it, your dietary restrictions shouldn't keep you from creating and enjoying great-tasting jam. In this section we tackle some of my favorite recipes using sugar-free sweeteners and substitutes. As in the previous chapters, there's a make-it-your-flavor section on pages 161–163, where I offer different herb and spice combinations to customize your sugar-free jam and fruit butters.

Sugar gives jam its characteristic mouthfeel and acts as a preservative. However, alternative sweeteners, such as honey or maple syrup, can be used as a flavor in these recipes with great results. Some preserving styles, such as fruit butters, are cooked for a long time, and therefore the natural sweetness of the fruit is condensed and no sweetener is necessary.

These jams are not as sweet as the recipes that use cane sugar. If you like a sweet jam, increase the sweetener ratio or experiment with adding other sweeteners.

Be aware that since these are sugar-free, you need to process the jars for the proper amount of time and with the recommended amount of citrus juice to ensure safe preservation.

Elevenses Peach Jam

Blackberry and Lavender Jam

Late-Summer Raspberry Jam

Sun-Gold Tomato Jam

Midnight Kitchen Wild Blueberry Jam

Umami Shiso Fine Plum Jam

Ginger Pear Jam

Big Apple Butter

Apricot Butter

Plum Butter

Ulysses's Fig Jam

ELEVENSES PEACH JAM

| *With black tea and wildflower honey—like peach sweet tea in a jar* |

Summer peaches are divine. This jam is perfect for a midmorning snack (called elevenses by the British), served on a scone with a hot cup of tea to accompany it. The slightly bitter and tannic taste of the tea pairs perfectly with the supersweet and mellow peaches. Honey serves as a nice finish and adds depth and sweetness to the jam. I recommend white peaches for this jam, but if you can find only yellow ones, they're a fine substitute.

This recipe is a two-day process, but the first day requires only about twenty minutes of preparation. The next day, it should take less than an hour to complete the cooking and processing.

Makes About Four 8-Ounce Jars or Two Pint Jars

INGREDIENTS

2¾ pounds white peaches (about 6 cups sliced)
4 tablespoons lemon juice
2 cups wildflower honey
3 tablespoons Ceylon tea
6 ounces water

Special Equipment
1 chinois sieve
1 candy thermometer

PREP

For the peaches:

Blanch the peaches in a pot of boiling water for about 1 minute. Refresh them by plunging them in an ice water bath and leaving them there for at least 30 seconds; this will help loosen the peel, and you should be able to easily pull it off with your hands. Halve the peaches and remove their pits, then cut the halves into slices.

Measure the fruit into a 6- to 8-quart nonreactive pot and add the lemon juice and honey. Stir well.

For the jars and lids:

Wash and rinse the jars; put them into a big stockpot; cover the jars with water and bring to a boil; turn off the heat. Let stand in hot water until you are ready to fill.

Bring the lids and rings to a boil; turn off the heat. Let stand in hot water until you are ready to screw them onto the jars.

Place a few metal spoons in the freezer for testing the consistency and gel of your jam later. You can also place them in a cup of ice water, if you prefer.

COOK

Bring the fruit to a simmer over medium-high heat until bubbles appear around the edges. Turn off the heat and pour this mixture into a glass bowl or heat-safe Tupperware container and cover with parchment paper or a lid. Refrigerate for at least 6 hours or overnight.

The next day, pour the fruit mixture through a sieve. Place the collected syrup in a 6- to 8-quart nonreactive pot. Reserve the peaches. Bring the syrup to a boil over high heat and cook on high heat for 20 minutes. If it starts to foam, skim the foam off the top and discard the foam.

Skim and return to a boil. The syrup will reach the gel stage at 221°F (105°C) on a candy thermometer, about 5 more minutes. If you don't have a thermometer, test the consistency by placing a teaspoon of the hot jam onto one of the prepped frozen spoons. Let it rest for a few minutes, then test the gel by tilting the spoon vertically; what is the consistency? If the jam runs loosely like syrup then it's not ready, but if it glides slowly along and starts to congeal, then it's ready.

As the jam cooks, brew the Ceylon tea with the water. Add the sliced peaches and the brewed tea to the cooked syrup. Bring to a boil over high heat and cook for 5 minutes, stirring gently and consistently. Check the set by using one of the prepped frozen spoons. Place it in the jam, and let it rest for 3 to 4 minutes. Then test the consistency by tilting the spoon vertically. If it runs loosely like syrup, then it's not done yet, but if it glides slowly along in a gloopy glob, then it's ready. If it is syrupy, bring it to a boil again for 1 to 5 minutes.

PRESERVE

See pages 29–30 for in-depth instructions on filling and processing the jars.

For this recipe, process the jars in a boiling water bath for 10 minutes.

TIPS

Pairs well with hard cheeses such as Mimolette or mild creamy blue cheese such as Fourmet d'Ambert; great on multigrain toast; delicious on thick Greek yogurt. See Make It Your Own on pages 161–163 for unique flavor combinations and ingredients you can use to customize your own flavor.

BLACKBERRY AND LAVENDER JAM

| *Tart fruit and floral lavender with a smooth honey sweetener* |

In this recipe, the lavender blossoms add perfume to tart blackberries. Honey tempers the tartness and adds a warm flavor, and although I recommend sage honey, you can use any variety that you prefer. This is one of our most popular flavors at the summer markets; we have frequent return customers who've become weekly consumers of Blackberry and Lavender Jam.

Blackberries are a ubiquitous American fruit, growing on low thorny bushes in yards, fields, and ditches throughout the States. Each berry is a cluster of berries, each with its own seed. When the fruit falls to the ground, each seed has the potential to become a new blackberry bush. It's easy to see how they spread!

Some people dislike seeds in their jam. If you wish to remove the seeds, simply run the jam through a food mill before adding the pectin. Use the lavender flowers instead of the leaves, as they'll be more flavorful.

Makes About Four 8-Ounce Jars or Two Pint Jars

INGREDIENTS

2 pounds fresh blackberries (about 4 cups)
2 teaspoons lavender blossoms
2 tablespoons lemon juice
2 cups sage honey

For the Gelling

See Chapter 3 for more information on pectin and calcium water
3 teaspoons calcium water
2 teaspoons pectin

PREP

For the blackberries:

Measure the berries and lavender into a 6- to 8-quart nonreactive pot and add the lemon juice and the proper amount of calcium water into the pan; stir well.

For the jars and lids:

Wash and rinse the jars; put them into a big stockpot; cover the jars with water and bring to a boil; turn off the heat. Let stand in hot water until you are ready to fill.

Bring the lids and rings to a boil; turn off the heat. Let stand in hot water until you are ready to screw them onto the jars.

Place a few metal spoons in the freezer for testing the consistency and gel of your jam later. You can also place them in a cup of ice water, if you prefer.

For the honey and pectin:

Measure the honey into a separate bowl or measuring cup and thoroughly mix the proper amount of pectin powder into the honey—using a fork helps to disperse the pectin into the honey. Set the honey-pectin mixture aside.

COOK

Bring the fruit mixture to a boil over medium-high heat. If it starts to foam, skim the foam off the top and discard the foam. Return to a boil again.

Pour the pectin-honey mixture into the boiling jam slowly and carefully, stirring as you add. Stir vigorously for 1 to 2 minutes to dissolve the pectin.

Return to a boil and remove from the heat. Skim off any and all foam that has formed on the top.

Pectin gels completely when thoroughly cool, so don't worry if your jam looks loose while still hot. To test, place a teaspoon of the hot jam onto one of the prepped frozen spoons; let it cool to room temperature (about 30 seconds) on the spoon. If it thickens up to the consistency desired, then the jam is ready. If not, mix in a little more pectin (½ teaspoon into ¼ cup sugar) and bring it to a boil again for 1 minute.

PRESERVE

See pages 29–30 for in-depth instructions on filling and processing the jars.

For this recipe, process the jars in a boiling water bath for 6 minutes.

TIPS

Pairs well with rich creamy Comté or Tête de Moine cheeses; great spooned onto a *panna cotta* dessert or in a tart with fresh cream; delicious on top of thick Greek yogurt. See Make It Your Own on pages 161–163 for unique flavor combinations and ingredients you can use to customize your own flavor.

LATE-SUMMER RASPBERRY JAM

| *A jam with raspberries and Lambrusco, perfect for keeping the dog days of summer—
particularly the heat and bounty of August—with you all year* |

What's better than a glass of cold, bubbly, deep-red Lambrusco and some raspberries on a hot summer day? This jam mimics the tart and bubbly flavors while using stevia as a sweetener. Stevia is a natural sweetener derived from the stevia leaf. Many sugar-free dieters prefer green stevia since it's less processed than other stevia. You can find green stevia in a well-stocked bulk section of many health food stores. Using the common white stevia is fine, however, and you can find it in many health food stores and gourmet bodegas.

Lambrusco is one of my favorite wines to drink in the summer, and I love drinking a glass with salads, hors d'oeuvres, and antipasti. If you're serving antipasti, use this jam on thin flatbread with hard sharp cheeses, such as Pecorino, accompanied by salty olives and wild boar salami.

Stevia has a strong flavor, unlike other alternative sweeteners like agave. If you don't enjoy the taste of stevia, you may substitute a milder sweetener, such as honey or agave.

Makes About Four 8-Ounce Jars or Two Pint Jars

INGREDIENTS
2 pounds fresh raspberries (about 4 cups)
2 tablespoons lemon juice
1 cup Lambrusco wine
1½ tablespoons stevia powder
½ cup water

FOR THE GELLING
See Chapter 3 for more information on pectin and calcium water
6 teaspoons calcium water
5 teaspoons pectin

PREP
FOR THE RASPBERRIES:
Measure the berries, lemon juice, and Lambrusco into a 6- to 8-quart nonreactive pot and add the proper amount of calcium water into the pan; stir well.

FOR THE JARS AND LIDS:

Wash and rinse the jars; put them into a big stockpot; cover the jars with water and bring to a boil; turn off the heat. Let stand in hot water until you are ready to fill.

Bring the lids and rings to a boil; turn off the heat. Let stand in hot water until you are ready to screw them onto the jars.

Place a few metal spoons in the freezer for testing the consistency and gel of your jam later. You can also place them in a cup of ice water, if you prefer.

COOK

Bring the fruit to a boil over medium-high heat. If it starts to foam, skim the foam off the top and discard the foam. Return to a boil again.

Bring the water to a boil. Put half the boiled water in a blender or food processor and carefully add the proper amount of pectin powder. Add the remaining boiled water. Vent the lid and blend 1 to 2 minutes, until all the powder is dissolved. Be careful: the pectin tends to clump on blades and in the container. Try to dissolve all of it.

Pour the pectin-water mixture into the boiling jam slowly and carefully, stirring as you add. Stir vigorously for 1 to 2 minutes to dissolve the pectin. Add the stevia and return to a boil. Remove from the heat. Skim off any and all foam that has formed on the top.

Pectin gels completely when thoroughly cool, so don't worry if your jam looks loose when still hot. To test, place a teaspoon of the hot jam onto one of the prepped frozen spoons; let it cool to room temperature (about 30 seconds) on the spoon. If it thickens up to the consistency desired, then the jam is ready. If not, mix in a little more pectin (½ teaspoon into ¼ cup sugar) and bring it to a boil again for 1 minute.

PRESERVE

See pages 29–30 for in-depth instructions on filling and processing the jars.

For this recipe, process the jars in a boiling water bath for 6 minutes.

TIPS

Pairs well with sweet and creamy Bonne Bouche and Bucheron; great served with almonds on maple crackers alongside Pâte de Campagne; delicious on top of ice cream or yogurt. See Make It Your Own on pages 161–163 for unique flavor combinations and ingredients you can use to customize your own flavor.

SUN-GOLD TOMATO JAM

| *With sweet sun-gold tomatoes and honey—the essence of tomatoes and summer in a jar* |

Sun-gold tomatoes are golden-colored tiny jewels of deliciousness, the sweetest, most flavorful tomato variety. These babies are amazingly fresh off the vine, and it will be hard to resist eating them all before you make this jam. Freshly picked tomatoes have a flavor that can never be replicated by their inferior winter cousins, grown hydroponically or in faraway factory farms. When I lived in Antarctica, I intensely craved the tangy, sweet and sour perfection of an earth-grown, sun-ripened tomato. The hydroponic tomatoes grown at the bottom of the Earth were like a sad celluloid clone, mimicking a tomato in appearance but lacking the magic of the real thing.

The tomatoes I use in Anarchy in a Jar's tomato jam are the real deal, grown with love and devotion by my friends at Brooklyn Grange rooftop farm in Long Island City. They're true urban tomatoes and the best I've ever tasted, but any freshly picked substitution you use in this recipe will pack the same punch. Farmers' markets will have sun-gold tomatoes from mid-June till late September—look for the bright-orange cherry tomatoes.

I never understood what tomato jam was until I had a taste of a friend's homemade variety and was wowed. I perfected this sugar-free recipe using supersweet sun-gold tomatoes and a little honey. Never use out-of-season tomatoes; it's not worth it, as the flavor will be bland.

Makes About Four 8-Ounce Jars or Two Pint Jars

INGREDIENTS

4 pounds sun-gold tomatoes (about 4 cups)
2 cups honey
1 jalapeño pepper, minced
½ teaspoon lemon zest
2 tablespoons lemon juice
2 tablespoons minced fresh ginger
1 teaspoon ground cumin
¼ teaspoon ground cinnamon
¼ teaspoon ground cloves
1 teaspoon salt

PREP

FOR THE TOMATOES:

Rinse and halve the tomatoes. Measure the tomatoes, honey, jalapeño pepper, lemon zest and juice, ginger, cumin, cinnamon, cloves, and salt into a 6- to 8-quart nonreactive pot. Stir to combine.

FOR THE JARS AND LIDS:

Wash and rinse the jars; put them into a big stockpot; cover the jars with water and bring to a boil; turn off the heat. Let stand in hot water until you are ready to fill.

Bring the lids and rings to a boil; turn off the heat. Let stand in hot water until you are ready to screw them onto the jars.

Place a few metal spoons in the freezer for testing the consistency and gel of your jam later. You can also place them in a cup of ice water, if you prefer.

COOK

Bring the mixture to a boil over high heat, stirring frequently; reduce the heat to medium and simmer for 1½ to 2 hours, stirring often to prevent scorching, until the consistency is thick and jamlike. To test, place a teaspoon of the hot jam onto one of the prepped frozen spoons; if liquid pools around the edges, return it to a boil and continue to cook until thickened.

PRESERVE

See pages 29–30 for in-depth instructions on filling and processing the jars.

For this recipe, process the jars in a boiling water bath for 12 minutes.

TIPS

Pairs well with firm, grassy cheeses such as Irish or New Zealand Cheddar and aged Gouda; great on a grilled cheese with sharp Cheddar; delicious on toast with tuna or whitefish. See Make It Your Own on pages 161–163 for unique flavor combinations and ingredients you can use to customize your own flavor.

MIDNIGHT KITCHEN WILD BLUEBERRY JAM

| *For the chef in all of us that loves the nice bite of Fernet,*
this jam is a unique and flashy concoction |

Many late nights, if you find yourself in the bar of a restaurant, particularly in New York or San Francisco, you'll find the chef, line cook, and occasional host finishing the long shift off with a shot of Fernet-Branca. San Francisco, in particular, has a love affair with the bitter and bold Italian *amaro*. You find it often served straight as a digestif or followed by a chaser of ginger ale or ginger beer.

When you eat this jam, the bold and complex flavors of *amaro*, vermouth, and ginger develop in the mouth and complement the tart wild blueberries.

This jam is a two-day process, but the first day's prep should take less than ten minutes to complete. The next day, it should take less than an hour to cook and process the jam.

Makes About Four 8-Ounce Jars or Two Pint Jars

INGREDIENTS

2¼ pounds wild blueberries (about 6 cups)
3 tablespoons lime juice
½ ounce Fernet-Branca
1 ounce Carpano Antica sweet vermouth
2 tablespoons finely diced fresh ginger
1 cup honey

FOR THE GELLING

See Chapter 3 for more information on pectin and calcium water
4 teaspoons calcium water
3 teaspoons pectin

PREP

FOR THE BLUEBERRIES:

Rinse the blueberries and remove stems. Measure the fruit into a glass bowl or plastic food-safe Tupperware container and add the lime juice. Stir well. Refrigerate overnight or up to 48 hours so that the lime juice is allowed to release the juice of the blueberries. When the juice is released, measure the blueberries mixture, Fernet-

Branca, sweet vermouth, and ginger into a 6- to 8-quart nonreactive pot and add the proper amount of calcium water into the pan; stir well.

FOR THE JARS AND LIDS:

Wash and rinse the jars; put them into a big stockpot; cover the jars with water and bring to a boil; turn off the heat. Let stand in hot water until you are ready to fill.

Bring the lids and rings to a boil; turn off the heat. Let stand in hot water until you are ready to screw them onto the jars.

Place a few metal spoons in the freezer for testing the consistency and gel of your jam later. You can also place them in a cup of ice water, if you prefer.

FOR THE HONEY AND PECTIN:

Measure the honey into a separate bowl or measuring cup and thoroughly mix the proper amount of pectin powder into it—using a fork helps to disperse the pectin into the honey. Set the mixture aside.

COOK

Bring the fruit mixture to a boil over medium-high heat. If it starts to foam, skim the foam off the top and discard the foam.

Pour the pectin-honey mixture into the boiling jam slowly and carefully, stirring as you add. Stir vigorously for 1 to 2 minutes to dissolve the pectin.

Return it to a boil and remove it from the heat. Skim off any and all foam that has formed on the top.

Pectin gels completely when thoroughly cool, so don't worry if your jam looks loose when still hot. To test, place a teaspoon of the hot jam onto one of the prepped frozen spoons; let it cool to room temperature (about 30 seconds) on the spoon. If it thickens up to the consistency desired, then the jam is ready. If not, mix in a little more pectin (½ teaspoon into ¼ cup sugar) and bring it to a boil again for 1 minute.

PRESERVE

See pages 29–30 for in-depth instructions on filling and processing the jars.

For this recipe, process the jars in a boiling water bath for 6 minutes.

TIPS

Pairs well with stinky Camembert; great on rye bread with pork rillettes and radicchio; delicious on top of thick Greek yogurt. See Make It Your Own on pages 161–163 for unique flavor combinations and ingredients you can use to customize your own flavor.

UMAMI SHISO FINE PLUM JAM

*| With shiso and maple syrup—say the name slowly, with attitude,
and it's "ooh-mommy-she's-so-fine" |*

I invented this recipe with my friend Cathy Erway, author of *The Art of Eating In* and the infamous blog *Not Eating Out in New York*, and a creatively fun cook to play with in the kitchen. We've cooked and eaten many a meal together; the sharing of food is sacrosanct among our group of friends.

Cathy invited me to a preservation experiment at her boyfriend's brewery, Sixpoint Craft Ales, and we had a blast getting a little wacky with the canning (it is a brewery, so we may have been a bit tipsy). This recipe is a riff on the classic Japanese umeboshi plum, which is a salt-fermented plum that has the herb shiso as a key ingredient.

Umami is one of the five basic tastes, together with sweet, sour, bitter, and salty—the word *umami* literally means "pleasant savory taste" in Japanese.

This combination of shiso, plum, maple syrup, and salt is a great example of umami. You know you've made it work if you get that pleasant furry feeling in your mouth when you eat this jam.

This jam is a two-day process, but the first day's prep should take less than ten minutes to complete. The next day, it should take less than an hour to cook and process the jam.

Makes About Four 8-Ounce Jars or Two Pint Jars

INGREDIENTS

3½ pounds plums (about 6 cups)
2 tablespoons finely chopped shiso
3 tablespoons lemon juice
1½ cups maple syrup
2 teaspoons sea salt

SPECIAL EQUIPMENT
1 candy thermometer

PREP

FOR THE PLUMS:

Rinse and halve the plums, discarding their pits. Measure the fruit into a glass bowl or plastic food-safe Tupperware container and add the shiso, lemon juice, maple syrup, and salt. Stir well. Refrigerate overnight or up to 48 hours so that the maple syrup and lemon juice are allowed to gently release the juice of the plums.

Once the juice is released, measure the fruit into a 6- to 8-quart nonreactive pot; stir well.

FOR THE JARS AND LIDS:

Wash and rinse the jars; put them into a big stockpot; cover the jars with water and bring to a boil; turn off the heat. Let stand in hot water until you are ready to fill.

Bring the lids and rings to a boil; turn off the heat. Let stand in hot water until you are ready to screw them onto the jars.

Place a few metal spoons in the freezer for testing the consistency and gel of your jam later. You can also place them in a cup of ice water, if you prefer.

COOK

Bring the plum mixture to a boil over high heat and cook for 5 minutes. Pour into a colander over a large bowl and stir to drain the juice from the plums. Reserve the plums. Return the juice to the pan and bring to a boil. Boil for 10 minutes until the juice has thickened and reduced, or when it's reached 221°F (105°C) on a candy thermometer.

Return the plums and any of their juices to the cooked juice and bring to a boil. Cook for 20 to 30 minutes, stirring frequently to prevent scorching. Gradually reduce the heat if the jam starts to stick and scorch; cook until the jam is no longer watery and seems nicely thickened. Keep a watchful eye and stir steadily for the last 5 to 10 minutes to prevent scorching. When the jam seems thickened and gelled, reduce the heat to low and test for consistency.

Jam gels completely when thoroughly cool, so don't worry if your jam looks loose when still hot. To test, place a teaspoon of the hot jam onto one of the prepped frozen spoons. Place the spoon back in the freezer, with the jam on it, for 3 to 4 minutes. Remove the spoon and test the gel by tilting the spoon vertically; what is the consistency? If the jam runs loosely like syrup then it's not done yet, but if it glides slowly along in a gloopy glob, then the jam is ready. If syrupy, bring it to a boil again for 1 to 5 minutes. This jam has a naturally looser consistency than some of the other jams in this book, but it should still be spreadable.

Once it is done, give it a last skim if there's any foam and turn off the heat.

PRESERVE

See pages 29–30 for in-depth instructions on filling and processing the jars.

For this recipe, process the jars in a boiling water bath for 6 minutes.

TIPS

Pairs well with fresh cheese like ricotta (recipe on page 206) or with grilled pork; great on vegetable or pork dumplings; delicious on seven-grain toast with Parmigiano-Reggiano and wild boar salami. See Make It Your Own on pages 161–163 for unique flavor combinations and ingredients you can use to customize your own flavor.

GINGER PEAR JAM

| *Spicy ginger and sweet pears with manuka honey meld into a perfect sugar-free treat* |

Pears are a great fruit to preserve, as their flavor becomes sweeter and their texture turns buttery when they're cooked, and they taste great with a variety of herbs and spices. Ginger is a natural fit and adds just enough spiciness to boost a pear's flavor and make your toast exciting. Feel free to add more ginger, if you are a fan. I recommend using sweet and rich manuka honey from New Zealand, but you may substitute any variety of honey you prefer.

Pairing pears with cheese is a classic combination, and this jam is great with sharp, hard cheeses such as Pecorino. Or try it with almond butter for a twist on the classic PB&J.

Makes About Four 8-Ounce Jars or Two Pint Jars

INGREDIENTS

2 pounds pears (about 6 medium pears; to equal 5 cups diced)
½ cup water
2 tablespoons lemon juice
2 cups manuka honey
2 tablespoons finely diced fresh ginger

FOR THE GELLING
See Chapter 3 for more information on pectin and calcium water
3 teaspoons calcium water
2 teaspoons pectin

SPECIAL EQUIPMENT
1 potato masher

PREP

FOR THE PEARS:
Rinse, peel, core, and dice the pears. Measure the fruit into a 6- to 8-quart nonreactive pot, add the water, lemon juice, and calcium water into the pan; stir well.

FOR THE JARS AND LIDS:
Wash and rinse the jars; put them into a big stockpot; cover the jars with water and bring to a boil; turn off the heat. Let stand in hot water until you are ready to fill.

Bring the lids and rings to a boil; turn off the heat. Let stand in hot water until you are ready to screw them onto the jars.

Place a few metal spoons in the freezer for testing the consistency and gel of your jam later. You can also place them in a cup of ice water, if you prefer.

FOR THE HONEY AND PECTIN:

Measure the honey into a separate bowl or measuring cup and thoroughly mix the proper amount of pectin powder into the honey—using a fork helps to disperse the pectin into the honey. Set the pectin-honey mixture aside.

COOK

Bring the pears to a boil over medium-high heat, covered with a lid, and cook for 30 minutes, until the pears begin to appear translucent. Remove the cover and add the ginger.

Mash the fruit with a potato masher until most of the fruit chunks have been broken apart. Do not mash into a smooth consistency; allow for a variety of sizes and textures in the fruit.

Return the pear mixture to a boil and stir frequently to prevent scorching.

Pour the pectin-honey mixture into the boiling jam slowly and carefully, stirring as you add. Stir vigorously for 1 to 2 minutes to dissolve the pectin.

Return to a boil and remove from the heat. Skim off any and all foam that has formed on the top.

Pectin gels completely when thoroughly cool, so don't worry if your jam looks loose while still hot. To test, place a teaspoon of the hot jam onto one of the prepped frozen spoons; let it cool to room temperature (about 30 seconds) on the spoon. If it thickens up to the consistency desired, then the jam is ready. If not, mix in a little more pectin (½ teaspoon into ¼ cup sugar) and bring it to a boil again for 1 minute.

PRESERVE

See pages 29–30 for in-depth instructions on filling and processing the jars.

For this recipe, process the jars in a boiling water bath for 6 minutes.

TIPS

Pairs well with punchy blue cheeses such as Stilton or hard cheese like Pecorino; great on sourdough toast and scones (recipe on page 203); delicious served with Coupole cheese, toasted walnuts, and endive. See Make It Your Own on pages 161–163 for unique flavor combinations and ingredients you can use to customize your own flavor.

BIG APPLE BUTTER

| *Sweet apples cooked down with cider and spices to create a thick and delicious buttery fruit spread* |

One of my jam pet peeves is calling the cooked down paste of fruit "butter." I can't tell you how many times people have asked me if it has dairy in it, and they can't be blamed, since using the term *butter* is a bit misleading. But alas, it's also a common enough food, and apple butter has so many fans that my attempts at changing the name have been useless. I even created a Facebook thread a few years ago to try to rename my apple butter, but people still want to call it apple butter. I decided following the Prince strategy of "artist-formally-known-as" seemed a little too complicated for a canned fruit that's the exact opposite of complicated.

Apple butter is a classic American treat, and so simple! Just apples and spices, if you wish, cooked down for a long time until all the water has evaporated and it's a thick and "buttery" texture. I call this Big Apple Butter as an ode to my city, often dubbed "the Big Apple." The nickname has a dubious history that started in the early twentieth century, but seems appropriate since New York has a long history of apple growing. There is still an incredible variety of heirloom apples grown around the state, and I suggest you use an assortment of any sweet varieties you like for this recipe. My favorite common ones that can be found in many grocery stores or at farmers' markets are Gala, Fuji, Winesap, McIntosh, and Yellow Delicious. My favorite heirloom varieties are Jonathan, Stayman Winesap, King David, Wickson Crabs, Sierra Beauty, Braeburn, Belle de Boskoop, Cox's Orange Pippin, Pink Pearl (really pink inside!), Jonagold, and Calville Blanc d'Hiver. You can find these heirloom varieties at many farmers' markets around the country starting in September, and I'm sure there are secret varieties you'll discover at your local market. Just ask the farmers for sweet apples for making apple butter; they're experts.

Apple butter is great to serve to kids, as it's a healthy sugar-free condiment that tastes great with peanut or almond butter and won't make them hyper, sugar-high monsters. And kids usually like its gentle flavor, even the picky ones. If your kids don't like spices, simply omit them, and the recipe will still taste great.

Makes About Six 8-Ounce Jars or Three Pint Jars

INGREDIENTS
6 pounds apples, cut into 1-inch chunks
6 cups apple cider

2 cups maple syrup
2 tablespoons lemon juice
1½ teaspoons ground cinnamon
½ teaspoon ground cloves
½ teaspoon ground cardamom

SPECIAL EQUIPMENT
1 food mill, strainer, or sieve

PREP

FOR THE APPLES:
Place the apple chunks, with skin and seeds still attached, in a 6- to 8-quart nonreactive pot. Add the apple cider.

FOR THE JARS AND LIDS:
Wash and rinse the jars; put them into a big stockpot; cover the jars with water and bring to a boil; turn off the heat. Let stand in hot water until you are ready to fill.

Bring the lids and rings to a boil; turn off the heat. Let stand in hot water until you are ready to screw them onto the jars.

Place a few metal spoons in the freezer for testing the consistency and gel of your jam later. You can also place them in a cup of ice water, if you prefer.

COOK

Bring the apples to a boil over high heat; boil for 30 to 40 minutes, until the apples are soft and pulpy, and the peels have separated from the flesh.

Run the mixture through a food mill to remove the peel and create an even texture. If you don't have a food mill, you can use a strainer or sieve, but the texture will not be as uniform.

Return the apple purée to the 6- to 8-quart nonreactive pot and add the maple syrup, lemon juice, cinnamon, cloves, and cardamom. Bring to a boil over high heat, then reduce the heat and stir often to prevent scorching. Cook for 2½ to 3 hours, or until the apple butter is thick, dark, and spreadable. To test, place a teaspoon of the hot apple butter onto one of the prepped frozen spoons; if liquid pools around the edges, return to a boil and continue to cook until thickened.

PRESERVE

See pages 29–30 for in-depth instructions on filling and processing the jars.

For this recipe, process the jars in a boiling water bath for 10 minutes.

TIPS

Pairs well with stinky Langres or Point Reyes blue cheese; great on a PB&J with almond butter; delicious on a sandwich with grilled turkey and Brie. See Make It Your Own on pages 161–163 for unique flavor combinations and ingredients you can use to customize your own flavor.

APRICOT BUTTER

| *Sweet apricots cooked down with orange and spices into a thick and delicious butter* |

Apricot butter is cooked very slowly until all the water has evaporated from the fruit and it has turned a lovely deep orange color. This recipe uses honey as a sweetener. If you cannot eat honey, the recipe will still taste great without it, but it will be significantly tarter in flavor. Oranges and spices boost the apricot's richness and add acidic tang.

Use the sweetest summer apricots you can find. In mid- to late July, the farmers' markets in New York and New England have small apricots, oozing with juice. Apricot butter is an easy and versatile way to make use of these fragile, delicious fruits.

Apricot butter is wonderful with toast and served as an accompaniment to roast chicken. I like eating it as a snack with crackers and almond butter.

Makes About Six 8-Ounce Jars or Three Pint Jars

INGREDIENTS
6 pounds apricots
3 oranges, juiced (to equal about 2 cups)
2 cups honey
1 tablespoon lemon juice
½ teaspoon ground cinnamon
½ teaspoon ground cloves
¾ teaspoon ground cardamom

SPECIAL EQUIPMENT
1 food mill or food processor or strainer or sieve

PREP
FOR THE APRICOTS:
Halve the apricots, remove their pits, and cut into 1½-inch pieces. Do not peel. Place the pieces into a 6- to 8-quart nonreactive pot, and add the orange juice, honey, lemon juice, cinnamon, cloves, and cardamom.

FOR THE JARS AND LIDS:

Wash and rinse the jars; put them into a big stockpot; cover the jars with water and bring to a boil; turn off the heat. Let stand in hot water until you are ready to fill.

Bring the lids and rings to a boil; turn off the heat. Let stand in hot water until you are ready to screw them onto the jars.

Place a few metal spoons in the freezer for testing the consistency and gel of your butter later. You can also place them in a cup of ice water, if you prefer.

COOK

Bring the fruit mixture to a boil over medium-high heat, reduce the heat, and cook until the fruit is very soft, about 20 minutes. Remove from the heat; purée the fruit and all its liquid in a food mill or food processor to remove the peel and create an even texture. If you don't have a food mill or food processor, you can use a strainer or sieve, but the texture will not be as uniform. Return the apricot purée to the 6- to 8-quart nonreactive pot and bring to a boil over high heat. Reduce the heat and cook for 2½ to 3 hours, or until the apricot butter is thick, dark, and spreadable. To test, place a teaspoon of the hot apricot butter onto one of the prepped frozen spoons; if liquid pools around the edges, return to a boil and continue to cook until thickened.

PRESERVE

See pages 29–30 for in-depth instructions on filling and processing the jars.

For this recipe, process the jars in a boiling water bath for 6 minutes.

TIPS

Pairs well with hard, dry and caramelly cheese such as Beehive Barely Buzzed, Vieille, or Podda Classico from Sicily; great on a roast chicken sandwich with fontina; delicious on top of thick Greek yogurt. See Make It Your Own on pages 161–163 for unique flavor combinations and ingredients you can use to customize your own flavor.

PLUM BUTTER

| *Sweet plums cooked down with tangerines and ginger make a thick and delicious butter* |

Plum butter is cooked very slowly until all the water has evaporated from the fruit and it's turned a lovely deep red color. This recipe uses honey as a sweetener. If you cannot eat honey, the recipe will still taste great without it, but it will be significantly more tart in flavor. Tangerines and ginger boost the pluminess while adding acid and richness.

Use the sweetest plums you can find, such as Damson or Mirabelle. In late September and early October, the farmers' markets in New York and New England are bursting with Damson plums that need to be cooked quickly before they become overripe.

Plum butter is wonderful with toast and served as an accompaniment to pork. I love using it as an alternative to Asian plum sauce.

Makes About Six 8-Ounce Jars or Three Pint Jars

INGREDIENTS
6 pounds plums
5 tangerines, juiced (to equal about 2 cups)
2 cups honey
2 tablespoons minced fresh ginger
1 tablespoon lemon juice
½ teaspoon ground cinnamon
½ teaspoon ground cloves

SPECIAL EQUIPMENT
1 food mill or food processor or strainer or sieve

PREP
FOR THE PLUMS:

Halve the plums, remove the pits, and cut into 1½-inch pieces. Do not peel. Place in a 6- to 8-quart nonreactive pot, and add the tangerine juice, honey, ginger, lemon juice, cinnamon, and cloves.

For the jars and lids:

Wash and rinse the jars; put them into a big stockpot; cover the jars with water and bring to a boil; turn off the heat. Let stand in hot water until you are ready to fill.

Bring the lids and rings to a boil; turn off the heat. Let stand in hot water until you are ready to screw them onto the jars.

Place a few metal spoons in the freezer for testing the consistency and gel of your butter later. You can also place them in a cup of ice water, if you prefer.

COOK

Bring the fruit mixture to a boil over medium-high heat, reduce the heat, and cook until the fruit is very soft, about 20 minutes. Remove from the heat; purée the fruit and all its liquid in a food mill or food processor to remove the peel and create an even texture. If you don't have a food mill or food processor, you can use a strainer or sieve, but the texture will not be as uniform. Return the plum purée to the 6- to 8-quart nonreactive pot and bring to a boil over high heat. Reduce the heat and cook for 2½ to 3 hours, or until the plum butter is thick, dark, and spreadable. To test, place a teaspoon of the hot plum butter onto one of the prepped frozen spoons; if liquid pools around the edges, return to a boil and continue to cook until thickened.

PRESERVE

See pages 29–30 for in-depth instructions on filling and processing the jars.

For this recipe, process the jars in a boiling water bath for 6 minutes.

TIPS

Pairs well with grassy cheese such as Hidden Springs Ocooch Mountain or the semifirm and salty Coinga Mahon Curado; great with pork dumplings and on a pulled pork sandwich; delicious on PB&J. See Make It Your Own on pages 161–163 for unique flavor combinations and ingredients you can use to customize your own flavor.

ULYSSES'S FIG JAM

*| Figs, honey, and wine will transport you to the land of the lotus-eaters
like Ulysses as you eat this perfect jam |*

I love everything about figs, but especially the smell of fresh figs in late summer and early autumn. I have a small fig tree that lives on my deck, and it explodes with fruit in September. I eagerly watch the figs develop and then ceremoniously eat the first fruit with a little drizzle of honey. As I lie in my hammock next to my small tree and breathe in the scent of figs, the sounds of the city fade and I'm transported to a taverna from my childhood in the backstreets of the island Tinos in Greece, where a huge gnarled fig tree grew over the entire café and the scent in autumn was heavy with the ripe musky fruit.

Ulysses (or Odysseus in Greek) was the legendary Greek king of Ithaca and hero of Homer's epic poem *The Odyssey*. *The Odyssey* describes Ulysses's fateful ten-year journey as he tries to return home after the Trojan War and reclaim his place as king of Ithaca. This jam would have been a fitting condiment for the lotus-eaters as they peacefully swooned on their island.

This recipe makes a jam that can be used as both a sweet and savory condiment. Figs are like tomatoes in that their pH level hovers near the danger zone of 4.6 (see Chapter 2). This means you have to add lemon juice to make them safe to process in a water bath, and you'll notice that you have to process them for a lot longer time than most of the recipes in this book.

Makes About Four 8-Ounce Jars or Two Pint Jars

INGREDIENTS
3 pounds fresh ripe figs (about 6 cups)
1 cup honey
3 tablespoons lemon juice
2 ounces red wine

SPECIAL EQUIPMENT
potato masher
food mill

PREP

FOR THE FIGS:

Rinse gently and cut the figs into eighths. Place 1 pound of the figs in a glass or stainless-steel bowl and add the honey, lemon juice, and wine; stir to combine. Allow the figs to macerate while you cook the other figs. Measure the remaining 2 pounds figs into a 6- to 8-quart nonreactive pot.

FOR THE JARS AND LIDS:

Wash and rinse the jars; put them into a big stockpot; cover the jars with water and bring to a boil; turn off the heat. Let stand in hot water until you are ready to fill.

Bring the lids and rings to a boil; turn off the heat. Let stand in hot water until you are ready to screw them onto the jars.

Place a few metal spoons in the freezer for testing the consistency and gel of your jam later. You can also place them in a cup of ice water, if you prefer.

COOK

Cover the 2 pounds figs with water. Cover the pot and bring to a boil over medium-high heat. Stir and reduce heat to medium; cover and cook for 5 more minutes. Uncover and mash the fruit with a potato masher so they release their juices. Cover, return to a boil and reduce to medium-low heat, and cook for about 25 minutes, stirring often, until the fruit is translucent and glossy.

Put the cooked figs through a food mill on the finest setting, then add them to the macerating figs mixture. If there are chunks of fruit left in the food mill, just add them to the rest of the figs.

Put this entire mixture back into the 6- to 8-quart nonreactive pot and bring to a boil over high heat. Reduce the heat to a simmer and mash with a potato masher. Simmer, stirring frequently to prevent scorching, for 20 to 25 minutes or until the jam is thickened.

This jam never really gels, but it becomes thickened. To test for consistency, place a teaspoon of the hot jam onto one of the prepped frozen spoons; let it cool to room temperature (about 30 seconds) on the spoon. If it thickens up to the consistency desired, then the jam is ready. If not, bring it to a boil again and cook for 5 more minutes. If it still doesn't gel, see Chapter 3 for more information on thickening (or "set") and how to achieve the best results.

PRESERVE

See pages 29–30 for in-depth instructions on filling and processing the jars.

For this recipe, process the jars in a boiling water bath for 12 minutes.

TIPS

Pairs well with hard sharp cheeses such as Pecorino, a nice smelly taleggio, or a sheep's milk cheese; great with antipasti of olives, olive oil crackers, and salami; delicious on scones or oat crackers. See Make It Your Own on pages 161–163 for unique flavor combinations and ingredients you can use to customize your own flavor.

MAKE IT YOUR OWN

Once you've mastered the basic recipes, become daring and develop your own. Start with a basic recipe, and then pick an herb, a spice, or an alcohol to add or substitute. The flavor chart below outlines my personal favorites, but feel free to create your own and go wild.

Elevenses Peach Jam
Instead of black tea, substitute:
orange zest (½ teaspoon)
ground nutmeg (2 teaspoons)
diced ginger (2 tablespoons, fresh)
vanilla bean (1 bean)

Blackberry and Lavender Jam
Instead of lavender, substitute:
rosemary (1 tablespoon, fresh)
Key lime zest and juice (¼ cup)
jalapeño peppers (2 tablespoons, fresh)
Cognac (2 ounces)
lemongrass (1 stem)

Late-Summer Raspberry Jam

Add one or more of the following:

cinnamon (1 teaspoon, ground)

sage (2 tablespoons, fresh)

Key lime zest and juice (¼ cup)

*Finger Lakes Raspberry Liqueur or
    Chambord (2 ounces)*

Sun-Gold Tomato Jam

Add one or more of the following:

whiskey (2 ounces)

cloves (1 teaspoon, ground)

rosemary (6 sprigs, fresh)

jalapeño peppers (2 tablespoons, fresh)

chervil (2 tablespoons, fresh)

ginger (2 tablespoons, fresh)

Midnight Kitchen Wild Blueberry Jam

Instead of Fernet-Branca and ginger,
substitute:

*whiskey (1 ounce) and cardamom
    (1 teaspoon, ground)*

*brandy (1 ounce) and sage (2 tablespoons,
    fresh)*

*orange blossom water (1 ounce) and cloves
    (2 teaspoons, ground)*

sake (1 cup) and lemongrass (2 stems)

Umami Shiso Fine Plum Jam

Add one or more of the following:

sea salt (½ teaspoon)

diced ginger (2 tablespoons, fresh)

Key lime zest and juice (¼ cup)

cloves (1 teaspoon, ground)

Grand Marnier (1 tablespoon)

Ginger Pear Jam

Instead of ginger, substitute:

rosemary (1 tablespoon, fresh)

jalapeño peppers (2 tablespoons, fresh)

gin (2 ounces)

lavender blossoms (1 tablespoon, dried)

Big Apple Butter

Instead of brandy, substitute:

bourbon (2 ounces)

maple syrup (2 ounces)

chamomile flower syrup (1 ounce)

Apricot Butter

Add one or more of the following:

sea salt (½ teaspoon)

vanilla bean (1 bean)

*Pop's Sour Cherry Liqueur (2 ounces,
    page 185)*

Plum Butter

Add one or more of the following:

*Cognac (1 ounce) and cardamom
    (1 teaspoon, ground)*

*Merlot (1 cup) and sage (2 tablespoons,
    fresh)*

*pomegranate molasses (1 ounce) and cloves
    (2 teaspoons, ground)*

sake (1 cup) and star anise (2 stems)

Ulysses's Fig Jam

Instead of wine, substitute:

port or brandy (1 ounce)

Ginger Syrup (1 ounce, page 190)

vanilla bean (1 bean)

7

PICKLED FRUIT, SYRUPS, AND SHRUBS

Let me start by saying these definitely aren't the recipes my mother taught me. This is what I think of as the "party chapter," where the fruit gets a little wild; pickled, preserved in salt, and strained into syrups and shrubs. Although archaic in tradition, the recipes here are hardly conventional. Pickled or salt-preserved fruits are sweet and tangy condiments that work great as accompaniments to sandwiches, meats, and cheeses; try serving the Pickled Strawberries as hors d'oeuvres at your next dinner party or jazz up roast lamb with Moroccan Preserved Lemons. You'll never look at cocktails in the same light after reading the recipes for syrups and shrubs, perfect for any get-together.

At the end of the chapter, look for the herb, spice, and fruit combinations under Make It Your Own on pages 196–197 if you'd like to create your own recipes for pickled fruits and liquors.

Aviation Pickled Pears

Pickled Strawberries

Pickled Watermelon Rind

Pickled Blueberries

Moroccan Preserved Lemons

Etruscan Preserved Figs

Candied Citrus Peel

Pop's Sour Cherry Liqueur

Lavender and Grapefruit Syrup

Ginger Syrup

Tart Attack Shrub

Summer Plum and Sour Cherry Shrub

AVIATION PICKLED PEARS

| *With crème de violette liqueur and juniper berries—pears are pickled to perfection* |

Have you ever tried an Aviation cocktail? If not, you should. It's delicious, with gin, lemon, and crème de violette liqueur. A few winter's ago, I decided to experiment with pickling fruit, in preparation for summer's bounty—plus, I was so bored with winter fruit. I thought of pickling the local late-autumn pears that farmers were still bringing to the markets. I thought of the crème de violette that was sitting on my liquor shelf. I had bought it thinking it would be a jam additive, but I never found the perfect jam in which to use it. It was one of those things that had to wait for its perfect partner. I started to imagine the delicious mixture of pear accented with the musty and seductive violet, balanced with juniper berries (the essence of gin!), one of my favorite spices. And lemon, of course. Voilà! Aviation in a jar was born.

Pickling fruit is a great way to preserve fruit for use in sandwiches or as hors d'oeuvres, as you would a sweet cucumber pickle or cornichon.

Makes Six 8-Ounce Jars

INGREDIENTS

4 pounds pears (about 8½ cups sliced)
5 cups sugar (2½ pounds)
2 cups apple cider or white wine vinegar
½ cup water
One 3-inch piece fresh ginger, diced
1 vanilla bean, split
2 ounces crème de violette liqueur
12 whole cloves
12 whole juniper berries
Peel of 1 lemon, sliced into 6 pieces
Peel of 1 orange, sliced into 6 pieces

PREP

FOR THE PEARS:

Rinse, peel, core, halve, and slice the pears.

FOR THE JARS AND LIDS:

Wash and rinse the jars; put them into a big stockpot; cover the jars with water and bring to a boil; turn off the heat. Let stand in hot water until you are ready to fill.

Bring the lids and rings to a boil; turn off the heat. Let stand in hot water until you are ready to screw them onto the jars.

COOK

In a 6- to 8-quart nonreactive pot, combine the sugar, vinegar, water, ginger, vanilla bean, and crème de violette. Bring to a boil over medium-high heat, stirring constantly. Reduce the heat and boil gently for 10 minutes. Remove and discard the vanilla bean (or save and add to a jar of sugar to make vanilla-infused sugar).

Place 2 whole cloves, 2 whole juniper berries, 1 lemon peel slice, and 1 orange peel slice into each jar. Pack the pear slices tightly into each jar, leaving a generous ½ inch of space at the top.

Ladle hot syrup into each jar to cover the pears, still leaving a ½ inch of space at the top of each jar. Remove any air bubbles, if necessary.

PRESERVE

See pages 29–30 for in-depth instructions on filling and processing the jars.

For this recipe, process the jars in a boiling water bath for 12 minutes.

TIPS

Pairs well with a sweet aged Comté or wacky balsamic and juniper-flavored Pecorino Ginepro; great on a grilled cheese with spicy Sottocenere cheese; delicious in a salad with candied walnuts and radicchio. See Make It Your Own on pages 196–197 for unique flavor combinations and ingredients you can use to customize your own flavor.

PICKLED STRAWBERRIES

| *Strawberries become savory with lemongrass, hibiscus, peppercorns, cloves, and star anise* |

Fresh summer strawberries need to be preserved in as many ways as possible. These pickles are sweet and savory, perfect for snacking or mixing into salads. Steve's Ice Cream in New York puts them on an ice cream sundae, and it's delicious!

Makes Six 8-Ounce Jars

INGREDIENTS
2¾ pounds strawberries (about 6 cups)
2 stems lemongrass
5 cups sugar (2½ pounds)
2 cups apple cider or white wine vinegar
½ cup water
2 tablespoons hibiscus flowers
12 whole cloves
12 whole black peppercorns
6 whole star anise
Peel of 1 lemon, sliced into 6 pieces

PREP
For the strawberries:
Rinse the berries and remove their hulls (green stems and leaves). Bruise the lemongrass with the back of a knife or mallet.

For the jars and lids:
Wash and rinse the jars; put them into a big stockpot; cover the jars with water and bring to a boil; turn off the heat. Let stand in hot water until you are ready to fill.

Bring the lids and rings to a boil; turn off the heat. Let stand in hot water until you are ready to screw them onto the jars.

COOK
In a 6- to 8-quart nonreactive pot, combine the sugar, vinegar, water, lemongrass, and hibiscus flowers. Bring to a boil over medium-high heat, stirring constantly. Reduce the heat and boil gently for 10 minutes.

Place 2 whole cloves, 2 whole black peppercorns, 1 star anise, and 1 lemon peel slice into each jar. Pack the whole strawberries tightly into each jar, leaving a generous ½ inch of space at the top.

Ladle hot syrup into each jar to cover the strawberries, still leaving a ½ inch of space at the top of each jar. Remove any air bubbles, if necessary.

PRESERVE

See pages 29–30 for in-depth instructions on filling and processing the jars.

For this recipe, process the jars in a boiling water bath for 12 minutes.

TIPS

Pairs well with bitey blue cheese such as Shropshire Blue or Cambozola or sweet, ripe Gorgonzola Dolce Artigianale (perfect for Valentine's Day hors d'oeuvres); great in a salad with blue cheese, endive, and candied pecans; delicious on a fried clam sandwich like the restaurant No. 7 in New York City serves. See Make It Your Own on pages 196–197 for unique flavor combinations and ingredients you can use to customize your own flavor.

PICKLED WATERMELON RIND

| *With hibiscus flowers and spices—watermelon rind is put to good use in these pickles* |

For this recipe, make sure that most of the pink flesh is removed (and eaten!) and only slight traces of the pink fruit are left on the watermelon rind. Cut away and discard the green peel, too. You'll be left with chunks of thick, white rind that seem inedible. But when they are cooked till they're translucent and infused with vinegar and spices, the pieces of rind become a delicious condiment that's great on sandwiches or used as you would use chutney with grilled or barbecued meats and vegetables.

Makes Six 8-Ounce Jars

INGREDIENTS

1 small watermelon (about 6 to 8 pounds)
8½ cups water
2 tablespoons coarse kosher salt
4 cups sugar (2 pounds)
2 cups apple cider vinegar
1 cinnamon stick
2 tablespoons hibiscus flowers
12 whole cloves
12 pink peppercorns
Peel of 1 lemon, sliced into 6 pieces

PREP

FOR THE WATERMELON:

Cut the watermelon pulp from the rind, leaving a thin layer of pink on the rind. Reserve the pulp for another use (such as eating while you make these pickles!). Cut the green outer skin from the rind and discard. Cut the white rind into 1 x ½-inch pieces.

FOR THE JARS AND LIDS:

Wash and rinse the jars; put them into a big stockpot; cover the jars with water and bring to a boil; turn off the heat. Let stand in hot water until you are ready to fill.

Bring the lids and rings to a boil; turn off the heat. Let stand in hot water until you are ready to screw them onto the jars.

COOK

Bring 8 cups water and the salt to a boil over medium-high heat and add the watermelon rind. Boil for 15 minutes, or until the rind softens and becomes slightly translucent. Drain the water and reserve the rind.

In a 6- to 8-quart nonreactive pot, combine the sugar, vinegar, ½ cup water, cinnamon stick, and hibiscus flowers. Bring to a boil over medium-high heat, stirring constantly. Reduce the heat and boil gently for 10 minutes. Remove the cinnamon stick and discard.

Place 2 whole cloves, 2 whole pink peppercorns, and 1 lemon peel slice into each jar. Gently place the watermelon rind pieces tightly into each jar, leaving a generous ½ inch of space at the top.

Ladle hot syrup into each jar to cover the rind, still leaving a ½ inch of space at the top of each jar. Remove any air bubbles, if necessary.

PRESERVE

See pages 29–30 for in-depth instructions on filling and processing the jars.

For this recipe, process the jars in a boiling water bath for 12 minutes.

TIPS

Pairs well with sweet and buttery cheese like Brillat-Savarin or on a fresh hot baguette with pungent Saint-Marcellin; great with barbecued baby back ribs; delicious in a prosciutto, melon, and arugula salad like the chef Paul Virant makes in Chicago. See Make It Your Own on pages 196–197 for unique flavor combinations and ingredients you can use to customize your own flavor.

PICKLED BLUEBERRIES

| *Blueberries are pickled into a savory treat with garlic and caraway* |

For this recipe, you can use either regular blueberries or wild ones.

I love to eat these with pork chops or in a sandwich with pastrami on rye bread.

Makes Six 8-Ounce Jars

INGREDIENTS

2 pounds blueberries (about 6 cups)
2 cups sugar (1 pound)
2 cups apple cider or white wine vinegar
½ cup water
1 cinnamon stick
6 cloves garlic, skins removed
2 tablespoons caraway seeds
Peel of 1 lemon, sliced into 6 pieces

PREP

FOR THE BLUEBERRIES:
Rinse the berries and remove their stems.

FOR THE JARS AND LIDS:
Wash and rinse the jars; put them into a big stockpot; cover the jars with water and bring to a boil; turn off the heat. Let stand in hot water until you are ready to fill.

Bring the lids and rings to a boil; turn off the heat. Let stand in hot water until you are ready to screw them onto the jars.

COOK

In a 6- to 8-quart nonreactive pot, combine the sugar, vinegar, water, and cinnamon stick. Bring to a boil over medium-high heat, stirring constantly. Reduce the heat and boil gently for 10 minutes. Remove and discard the cinnamon stick.

Place 1 clove garlic, ¼ teaspoon caraway seeds, and 1 lemon peel slice into each jar. Pack whole blueberries tightly into each jar, leaving a generous ½ inch of space at the top.

Ladle hot syrup into each jar to cover the blueberries, still leaving a ½ inch of space at the top of each jar. Remove any air bubbles, if necessary.

PRESERVE

See pages 29–30 for in-depth instructions on filling and processing the jars.

For this recipe, process the jars in a boiling water bath for 12 minutes.

TIPS

Pairs well with pork and roast turkey; great as a condiment on sandwiches; delicious with olive oil crackers and Brie. See Make It Your Own on pages 196–197 for unique flavor combinations and ingredients you can use to customize your own flavor.

MOROCCAN PRESERVED LEMONS

| Meyer lemons are pickled in a brine of salt and their juice, plus a few spices to make them extra delicious |

Preserved lemons, or lemon pickles, are a condiment that I use every day. You can always find a big jar full of them in my fridge, or fermenting on my shelf. They've got a light, clean flavor that's a wonderful addition to any meal. Plus, they're rich in lactic-acid-producing bacteria, so they are healthy.

Preserved lemons are a condiment that's common in South Indian and North African cuisine, especially Moroccan. Diced, quartered, halved, or whole lemons are pickled in a brine of lemon juice and salt; spices can be included as well. The lemons ferment at room temperature for a few days or weeks, then are eaten immediately or refrigerated indefinitely. The pulp of the preserved lemon can be used in stews and sauces, but it's the peel that's the jewel of this recipe. The flavor is mildly tart, delicately briny, and intensely lemony. The salt fermentation softens the bitterness of the peel and infuses it with a delicious bite. You can slice, chop, or mince the lemon pickle as you like for the texture of a dish; you can use the pulp, if you wish, but it can be a bit mushy.

I love preserved lemons in a salad dressing with fresh garlic, mustard, olive oil, and a dash of apple cider vinegar, or mixed into Blood Marys.

I highly recommend using Meyer lemons for this recipe, because they're so delicious and light in flavor, but regular lemons are acceptable to use if necessary; just make sure they are juicy and fresh. Always use organic or unsprayed lemons if possible, since you're going to be eating the skin, too, in this recipe. If they're small, eight to ten lemons at a time should work, but be sure to buy two or three extra lemons for juicing a couple days later, in case you need to add additional liquid to keep the lemons in the jar submerged while they macerate and ferment. It's best to use good salt. Kosher will do fine, but nice big French gray sea salt is my favorite. Don't use ordinary table salt or anything that's iodized, as it will impart a harsh, chemical taste and can affect the color and texture as well. Feel free to experiment with other citrus fruit, such as Key limes or grapefruit.

Makes One 32-Ounce Jar or One Quart Jar

INGREDIENTS

8 to 10 Meyer lemons

8 to 10 tablespoons kosher salt (1 tablespoon per lemon), plus more for the jar

3 tablespoons freshly squeezed lemon juice, if necessary

Add some or all of the following:

1 tablespoon dried crushed chili pepper

1 tablespoon coriander seeds

1 cinnamon stick

1 fresh bay leaf

SPECIAL EQUIPMENT

1 quart canning jar (32 ounces)

PREP

FOR THE LEMONS:

Scrub the lemons with a vegetable brush or scrubber and dry them off.

If any of the lemons have a hard stem on one end, cut it off. To cut a big *X* shape into the lemon, place the nonstem end of a lemon on top, slice lengthwise downward, making a deep cut, but stopping about 1 inch from the bottom; make another downward slice, perpendicular to the first slice, so you've cut the lemon into an *X* shape but have left the bottom still attached. Repeat for all the lemons.

FOR THE JARS AND LIDS:

I recommend using a large 32-ounce jar, either a pretty Mason-style jar or a Le Parfait–style jar with a hinged lid and snap lock. You want these lemons to look sexy when they're sitting on your counter.

Wash and rinse the jar; put it into a big stockpot; cover the jar with water and bring to a boil; turn off the heat. Let stand in hot water until you are ready to fill.

Bring the lid and ring to a boil; turn off the heat. Let stand in hot water until you are ready to screw it onto the jar.

COOK

Pack the coarse salt into each lemon where you made the incisions. Don't be skimpy with the salt; really get your hands into it. Use gloves if you might have any cuts on your hands, as the lemon and salt will make them sting.

PRESERVE

Place the salt-filled lemons in the clean, large glass jar with a tight-fitting lid: Begin with 1 lemon with the cut side up and then stuff the next lemon cut side down into the opening of the first lemon, and really shove it in there to release the juice and salt. Throw some extra salt in as you go. Now add the rest of the lemons, cramming each one in there hard and pressing them down as you go. Keep throwing salt in there with each level. If you want to use spices, add them now as you layer the lemons.

Press the lemons firmly in the jar to help release the juices. Cover and let stand overnight.

The next day, press the lemons down again, encouraging them to release more juice as they start to soften. You may have to repeat this for a few days, until the lemons are completely covered with liquid. If your lemons aren't very juicy, add enough freshly squeezed lemon juice until they are submerged. I find that Meyer lemons are quite juicy and don't need added juice, but regular lemons may.

After 4 or 5 weeks, when the lemons are pliable and soft, you can start using them. At this point, store the lemons in the refrigerator, and they'll keep for at least 6 months, if not a year. You can rinse the lemons before you eat them to remove excess salt.

TIPS

How do you use them? They're great in a variety of dishes, so please experiment. Before cooking with one, extract it from the liquid and rinse it; cut it in half and scrape out any seeds or pulp, then chop the remaining peel into strips or a small dice, depending on the recipe you're using.

Pairs well with lamb and couscous; great as a condiment for grilled vegetables and meat; delicious with oily fish, such as trout, bluefish, or mackerel. See Make It Your Own on pages 196–197 for unique flavor combinations and ingredients you can use to customize your own flavor.

ETRUSCAN PRESERVED FIGS

| *With brandy and bay leaf—you can eat the figs and use the syrup in sodas, cocktails, and desserts* |

On a late summer evening in August, as I sat in the backyard of one of my favorite neighborhood bars in Carroll Gardens, Brooklyn, I was delighted to look up and see the classic trident-shaped leaves of a fig towering over the garden, with ripe fruits dangling just out of reach. I recalled the sweet and musky scent of the woods near my uncle's house in Umbria, Italy, where fig trees grew all along the path.

My Italian family name is Calamandrei, a somewhat obscure and ancient family name that can be traced to the Etruscans who occupied Italy before the Romans. The Italians call figs preserved in syrup *fichi sciroppati*, and it's the most basic way to preserve fruit—I'm sure some form of it was being made when my ancestors roamed around those same hills in Umbria.

Figs are a special fruit, somehow redolent with heavenly charm. Associated with Mediterranean climates (and in the United States, with warmer climates such as California and the South) where they grow so well, it's hard to believe they grow in Brooklyn, too! While not as spectacular as their Mediterranean cousins, New York figs are still delicious. Preserved in syrup, these figs make a delicious treat in midwinter.

Figs often have two harvests, one early in the summer and one just before autumn descends. In the Northeast, this often means that the frost comes before the figs are ripe—a travesty. Our volatile climate also means that figs can go from semiripe to overripe in a day. This recipe works well for almost-ripe figs, but stay away from ones that are completely unripe, as they need extra care to be edible.

Figs are like tomatoes in that their pH level hovers near the danger zone of 4.6 (see "Basics" chapter, page 18). This means you have to add lemon juice to make them safe to process in a water bath, and you'll notice that you have to process them for much longer than most of the recipes in this book.

Makes About Four 8-Ounce Jars or Two Pint Jars

INGREDIENTS
2½ pounds almost-ripe figs
2 cups water
1 cup brandy

1¼ cups sugar (about ½ pound)
1 lemon, zested in long, wide strips and juiced (to
equal 2 tablespoons juice)
2 fresh bay leaves, optional

PREP

FOR THE FIGS:

Wash the figs very gently, taking care to not
break their skins. Cut off their stems along
with a bit of the fruit from that end and
make a small slit at the bottom of the figs.

FOR THE JARS AND LIDS:

Wash and rinse the jars; put them into a big
stockpot; cover the jars with water and bring
to a boil; turn off the heat. Let stand in hot
water until you are ready to fill.

Bring the lids and rings to a boil; turn off
the heat. Let stand in hot water until you are
ready to screw them onto the jars.

COOK

To blanch the figs so they become softened,
place them in a pot and cover with water.
Bring to a boil over medium-high heat. Boil
for 5 minutes, then drain. If the figs are
semiripe, repeat this step 3 times, draining
the water and bringing to a boil with fresh
water each time. Poke the figs to see if

they've softened a bit. If not, repeat process up to 2 more times.

Using a slotted spoon, lift the figs out of the water and place in a bowl. Carefully
pour out the hot water. Give the pot a quick rinse (figs can produce a sticky resin
that's annoying to clean).

Combine the water, brandy, sugar, lemon zest, and bay leaves, if using. Bring to a
boil and add the figs; continue cooking, until the liquid becomes slightly viscous and
syrupy and the figs begin to glisten. Stir very gently, taking care to not break the figs.

PRESERVE

Pour in the lemon juice and stir to combine; fill the jars, leaving ½ inch of space at the top.

See pages 29–30 for in-depth instructions on filling and processing the jars.

For this recipe, process the jars in a boiling water bath for 30 minutes.

TIPS

Protect your hands with plastic gloves while preparing the figs, as the white liquid near the stems is sticky and can irritate the skin.

Pairs well with strong cheeses such as Gorgonzola Dolce or blue cheese such as Jasper Hill's Blue Moon; great spooned onto toast with mascarpone; delicious on top of ice cream or yogurt. See Make It Your Own on pages 196–197 for unique flavor combinations and ingredients you can use to customize your own flavor.

CANDIED CITRUS PEEL

| *For baking, gifts, or a sweet snack, these candied citrus peels are delicious and diverse* |

As a child, my mother would make fruitcake for my father every year (his favorite Christmas treat), and I would eat the candied citrus peel while I "helped" make the cake. I loved the flavor: sweet and tart, and just a little bitter.

Any citrus fruit can be substituted for the Ruby Red grapefruit, Seville oranges, and Meyer lemons; use spicy Rangpur limes or woodsy Bergamot oranges if you can find them. This recipe calls for muscovado sugar, a minimally refined cane sugar that's especially wonderful for baking and dusting. Made by pressing the sugarcane to release the juice and then cooking it slightly before allowing it to dry, muscovado sugar retains much of the flavor of the original cane. It has a high molasses content, moist texture, and deep, rich flavor.

Makes About Two Cups

INGREDIENTS
2 Ruby Red grapefruits
3 Seville oranges
4 Meyer lemons
1 cup granulated sugar (½ pound)
1 cup water
1½ cups light muscovado sugar, for rolling and dusting

Special Equipment
1 food processor

PREP
For the citrus fruit:
Using a sharp paring knife, make 6 slits along the curve of each grapefruit, orange, and lemon from top to bottom, cutting through the peel but not into the fruit's white pith or flesh. Using your fingers, gently remove the peel. Reserve the fruit flesh for another use, or eat it right away. Using the sharp paring knife, remove any excess white pith from each piece of peel and discard. I like to scrape it off with the knife's edge; or use a spoon to scrape and scoop it out.

Slice each piece of peel lengthwise into ¼-inch-wide strips.

COOK

In a medium pot of cold water, add the peels and bring to a boil over medium-high heat, then drain. Add more cold water to cover the fruit peels; bring to a boil again, then drain. Repeat twice. With a slotted spoon, transfer the peel to a wire rack set over a rimmed baking sheet; spread in a single layer to dry slightly, about 15 minutes.

PRESERVE

In a medium saucepan, bring 1 cup granulated sugar and 1 cup water to a boil over high heat, stirring to dissolve the sugar. Add the peel strips and return to a boil. Reduce the heat to low, cover, and simmer for 1 hour, until the rinds become translucent and jewel-like in appearance. Stir occasionally to prevent scorching, taking care to not damage the peels.

With a slotted spoon, transfer the peels to a wire rack or baking sheets lined with parchment paper, separating the strips as needed so they don't stick together.

Let the peel strips dry 3 hours or up to overnight. The next day, process the muscovado sugar in a food processor until fine. Toss the sticky pieces of peel in this sugar to coat. Shake the peels gently and return to the cookie sheets. Dry them for at least another 4 hours or up to overnight before placing in an airtight container for storage.

I like to give them as gifts, packaged in decorative jars with a little ribbon to accent the color of the peels.

TIPS

Instead of covering the rinds in sugar, dip them in chocolate and allow to dry for a few hours or overnight before storing or packaging. See Make It Your Own on pages 196–197 for unique flavor combinations and ingredients you can use to customize your own flavor.

POP'S SOUR CHERRY LIQUEUR

| *With brandy, vodka, sour cherries, and spices—add this boozy syrup to cocktails or soda water, or spoon it over ice cream* |

I have a vivid memory of returning home early from a sleepover when I was a preteen and happening upon my parents and their friends playing poker and drinking my father's homemade sour cherry liqueur. They were boisterous and probably a little drunk, and in a secret adult world unknown to me. My auntie Gioia was winning, and in her victorious mood, she gave me a sip of her drink. The flavor was intoxicating—I still remember the taste of cherries and brandy on my tongue.

My father never uses recipes or measurements of any kind, so when I asked him about that legendary sour cherry liqueur, his instructions were "throw some cherries in a bottle, add some brandy, maybe some vodka, you could use a few spices if you want, let all that stuff sit for a while, maybe a few months." I experimented and worked out the ratios, and this recipe mimics my memory of that long-ago taste to perfection.

Makes One 64-Ounce Jar

INGREDIENTS
1½ pounds sour red or Morello cherries (about 4 cups)
5 whole cloves
1 vanilla bean, split
1½ cups sugar (¾ pound)
2½ cups 100-proof vodka
1 cup brandy

SPECIAL EQUIPMENT
1 half-gallon jar (64 ounces)
1 piece cheesecloth

PREP
FOR THE CHERRIES:
Rinse the cherries and puncture each one with a small slice at the bottom to open the cherries but not halve or separate them; you want the pits to stay in the cherries.

For the jar and lid:
Wash and rinse the jar and closure.

PRESERVE

Place the cloves and vanilla bean in the jar, then layer the fruit and sugar by measuring a third of the cherries in the jar and adding ½ cup sugar on top. Add the next third of the cherries and the next ½ cup sugar, finishing with the last third of both. Pour the vodka and brandy in the jar, making sure all the fruit is completely submerged. Stir the mixture with a few vigorous stirs to dissolve some of the sugar, put the lid on the jar, and store in a cool, dry, dark place, such as a cupboard or closet.

For the first 2 weeks, shake the jar gently once a day to dissolve the sugar. After the sugar has dissolved, leave the jar in a dark cupboard or closet for 2 months to allow the flavors to develop.

After the first 2 months, taste a sip: does it taste amazing and flavorful? If not, let it rest longer, up to another month. When the mixture tastes to your liking, strain the cherries, pits, and spices through a cheesecloth, and funnel the filtered liqueur into bottles of your choice. Voilà! Gorgeous blood-red liqueur, preferably served in goblets to your most discerning of friends or enemies.

TIPS

Use only sour cherries; Bing or other sweet varieties will not work with this recipe. Make sure to leave the pits in; they add a delicious and subtle bitter-almond flavor.

Use only 100-proof vodka.

Try this liqueur in a cocktail that calls for cherry liqueur, such as a Singapore Sling with gin, lime juice, Bénédictine herbal liqueur, and brandy; great stirred into soda water; delicious on top of ice cream or yogurt. See Make It Your Own on pages 196–197 for unique flavor combinations and ingredients you can use to customize your own flavor.

LAVENDER AND GRAPEFRUIT SYRUP

| *With Ruby Red grapefruit and lavender blossoms—this tart and*
floral syrup makes a refreshing homemade soda |

There are a few different artisanal-soda syrup makers in New York City, and they inspired this recipe. I share my jam-making facility with Anton Nocito of P&H Soda Company, and our herbaceous and fruity cooking fills the alley outside with enchanting smells. We started our businesses around the same time, and I'm always inspired by his creative inventions. Another soda company is Brooklyn Soda Works, which sells its fresh sodas at many of the outdoor markets where I sell my jam. My favorite flavor to drink on a hot summer day is grapefruit. Anton makes a really special grapefruit and chamomile syrup that's delicious, and Brooklyn Soda Works makes a grapefruit and jalapeño soda for Smorgasburg Market in Williamsburg, Brooklyn, that I'm addicted to.

This is my own rendition using lavender flowers and pink grapefruits, and I make it at home to quench the thirst of guests but not get them wasted during summer afternoon barbecues and winter house parties.

Makes About Three 8-Ounce Jars

INGREDIENTS
2 Ruby Red grapefruits (to equal 2 cups juice)
2 cups sugar (1 pound)
2 cups water
3 tablespoons fresh or dried lavender flowers
2 tablespoons lemon juice
½ teaspoon salt

SPECIAL EQUIPMENT
1 piece cheesecloth, jelly bag, or coffee filter

PREP
FOR THE FRUIT:
Rinse and zest the grapefruits. Juice them with a juicer or with your hands; strain the juice to remove any seeds.

FOR THE JARS AND LIDS:

Wash and rinse the jars; put them into a big stockpot; cover the jars with water and bring to a boil; turn off the heat. Let stand in hot water until you are ready to fill.

Bring the lids and rings to a boil; turn off the heat. Let stand in hot water until you are ready to screw them onto the jars.

COOK

Place the grapefruit zest and juice, sugar, water, lavender, lemon juice, and salt in a medium saucepan. Bring to a boil over medium-high heat. Remove from the heat and let macerate for 1 hour.

Strain the hot syrup through double layers of cheesecloth, a jelly bag, or a coffee filter. Discard the dry pulp.

If not preserving the syrup, place it in an airtight container and keep it refrigerated until ready to use, up to 2 weeks.

PRESERVE

See pages 29–30 for in-depth instructions on filling and processing the jars.

For this recipe, process the jars in a boiling water bath for 10 minutes.

TIPS

To use, you may want to transfer the syrup to a pretty bottle. Open the jars, and using a funnel, transfer the syrup into the bottle for use at your next dinner party or cocktail soiree. You must refrigerate this bottle after opening the seal of the jars.

To serve, fill a 16-ounce glass with ice cubes and add 1½ ounces of the syrup; top with seltzer and stir to combine.

Try this syrup in a cocktail that calls for citrus syrup; great stirred into tonic water with a splash of Campari. See Make It Your Own on pages 196–197 for unique flavor combinations and ingredients you can use to customize your own flavor.

GINGER SYRUP

| *With fresh ginger—inspired by Morris Kitchen's lovely Brooklyn-made syrup* |

Kari Morris and her brother Tyler started Morris Kitchen a few years back, and they produce artisanal syrups to use in cocktails and a myriad of dishes. Using their recipe as inspiration, I developed my own interpretation.

This syrup is simple to make and has a nice spicy bite to it from the ginger. It's great with soda water or stirred into cocktails. Kari also recommends adding it to dishes like the dressing for a carrot salad or baked butternut squash and mixed into desserts like lemon curd. Their Web site offers great suggestions for incorporating syrups into your next meal.

Makes About Three 8-Ounce Jars

INGREDIENTS

Three 3-inch pieces fresh ginger
2 cups sugar (1 pound)
2 cups water
2 tablespoons lemon juice
½ teaspoon salt

Special Equipment
1 piece cheesecloth, jelly bag, or coffee filter
1 juicer or food processor

PREP

For the fruit:
Chop the ginger in a juicer or food processor, until it resembles a thick ginger sludge.

For the jars and lids:
Wash and rinse the jars; put them into a big stockpot; cover the jars with water and bring to a boil; turn off the heat. Let stand in hot water until you are ready to fill.

Bring the lids and rings to a boil; turn off the heat. Let stand in hot water until you are ready to screw them onto the jars.

COOK

Place the ginger sludge, sugar, water, lemon juice, and salt in a medium saucepan. Bring to a boil over medium-high heat. Remove from the heat and let macerate for 1 hour.

Strain the hot syrup through a double layer of cheesecloth, a jelly bag, or a coffee filter. Discard the dry pulp.

If not preserving the syrup, place it in an airtight container and keep it refrigerated until ready to use, up to 2 weeks.

PRESERVE

See pages 29–30 for in-depth instructions on filling and processing the jars.

For this recipe, process the jars in a boiling water bath for 10 minutes.

TIPS

To use, you may want to transfer the syrup to a pretty bottle. Open the jars, and using a funnel, transfer the syrup into the bottle for use at your next dinner party or cocktail soiree. You must refrigerate this bottle after opening the seal of the jars.

To serve, fill a 16-ounce glass with ice cubes and add 1½ ounces of the syrup; top with seltzer and stir to combine.

Try it in a cocktail that calls for ginger syrup, such as a Dark and Stormy with 2 ounces rum, ½ ounce ginger syrup, 1 ounce lime juice, and 3 ounces seltzer; great stirred into soda water with a dash or two of bitters. See Make It Your Own on pages 196–197 for unique flavor combinations and ingredients you can use to customize your own flavor.

TART ATTACK SHRUB

| *Old-fashioned vinegar-based syrup with rhubarb and lime—*
for those who love a good tart kick |

Vinegar soda? Sounds gross, I know. But when you make shrubs, the acidity mellows as the vinegar is mixed with sugar and diluted with bubbly water or cocktails.

Shrubs date back to Colonial times, but they are becoming trendy once again. I find them popping up all over town in one form or another. A hot new spot in the West Village has been offering a Dark and Stormy drizzled with balsamic vinegar.

There are two successful ways to make shrubs. One involves cooking and is quick and simple: make the syrup out of sugar, water, and fruit, and then add vinegar. The other option is to cold-brew the shrub. This method results in a fresher and brighter-tasting shrub, and is a fun alternative to cooking over a hot stove during the summer. The only down side is that it takes a few days. This recipe requires you to cold-brew the shrub, but turn to the next recipe if you would like to make the cooked version.

Makes About Three 8-Ounce Jars

INGREDIENTS
2 stalks rhubarb (to equal 1 cup diced)
4 limes (to equal about ½ cup juice)
1½ cups sugar (¾ pound)
1 cup apple cider vinegar

Special Equipment
1 piece cheesecloth, jelly bag, or coffee filter

PREP
For the rhubarb:
Rinse and dice the rhubarb; make sure to use a sharp knife as rhubarb is stringy and it takes a strong chop to separate. Juice the limes in a juicer or by hand; strain the juice to remove any seeds. Measure the rhubarb into a glass bowl or plastic food-safe Tupperware container and add the lime juice and sugar. Stir to combine.

Refrigerate overnight or up to 48 hours to macerate and allow the rhubarb to release its juice. After about 12 hours, the fruit should be surrounded by a syrupy juice. Stir the mixture every few hours to dissolve the sugar.

BREW

Once the juice is released, strain the syrup through a cheesecloth, a jelly bag, or a coffee filter, pressing lightly on the rhubarb to release as much juice as possible. Make sure you wipe any undissolved sugar from the bowl and place it into the syrup.

Add the vinegar, whisking to combine, until the sugar is dissolved and the syrup is smooth.

PRESERVE

Pour the syrup through a funnel into a clean jar or bottle. Cap the jar, give it a shake, and place it in the refrigerator.

Now the shrub is almost done. Shake it every few days in case some sugar has settled on the bottom. The acid in the juice and vinegar will eventually dissolve the sugar, and your syrup will be smooth. Shrubs taste better after a few weeks, as the yeast and acid start to get feisty and produce a light carbonation and richer flavor.

Keep refrigerated; the shrub should last up to a year in the fridge.

TIPS

To serve, fill a 16-ounce glass with ice cubes and add 1½ ounces of the syrup; top with seltzer and stir to combine.

Try it in a cocktail such as a Rhubarb Gimlet by adding 2 ounces gin to 1 ounce of Tart Attack Shrub, garnish with a lime; great stirred into soda water with a dash of orange bitters. See Make It Your Own on pages 196–197 for unique flavor combinations and ingredients you can use to customize your own flavor.

SUMMER PLUM AND SOUR CHERRY SHRUB

| *With plums, sour cherries, and balsamic vinegar—a hip shrub for summer afternoons* |

This shrub recipe is sweet, sour, and tart all at once. I love the flavors of plum and sour cherry together—so refreshing and addictive. Balsamic vinegar is sweet and tastes great with this flavor combination, but you can experiment with other vinegars if you're curious.

This recipe calls for you to make the shrub by cooking it. You can also cold-brew shrubs (see previous recipe).

Makes About Three 8-Ounce Jars

INGREDIENTS
1 pound plums (about ¾ cup)
½ pound sour cherries (about 1½ cups)
2 cups balsamic vinegar
½ cup lemon juice
2½ cups sugar (1¼ pounds)

SPECIAL EQUIPMENT
1 potato masher
1 piece cheesecloth, jelly bag, or coffee filter

PREP
FOR THE FRUIT:
Pit and halve the plums and cherries. Place the fruit into a pint-size jar or nonreactive bowl and lightly crush using a fork or potato masher. Add the vinegar and lemon juice; stir to combine. Cover and refrigerate for at least 24 hours, occasionally shaking the jar or stirring the contents of the bowl to distribute the juices.

The next day, combine the fruit and its liquid with the sugar in a 6- to 8-quart nonreactive pot.

FOR THE JARS AND LIDS:
Wash and rinse the jars; put them into a big stockpot; cover the jars with water and bring to a boil; turn off the heat. Let stand in hot water until you are ready to fill.

Bring the lids and rings to a boil; turn off the heat. Let stand in hot water until you are ready to screw them onto the jars.

COOK

Bring the fruit to a boil over medium-high heat. Remove from the heat and let the mixture macerate for 1 hour. Strain the syrup through double layers of cheesecloth, a jelly bag, or a coffee filter. Let drip for as long as it takes to fully render the juice. Discard the dry pulp.

If you are not preserving the syrup, place it in an airtight container and keep refrigerated until ready to use, up to 2 weeks.

PRESERVE

See pages 29–30 for in-depth instructions on filling and processing the jars.

For this recipe, process the jars in a boiling water bath for 10 minutes.

TIPS

To use, you may want to transfer the syrup to a pretty bottle. Open the jars, and using a funnel, transfer the syrup into the bottle for use at your next dinner party or cocktail soiree. You must refrigerate this bottle after opening the seal of the jars.

To serve, fill a 16-ounce glass with ice cubes and add 1½ ounces of the syrup; top with seltzer and stir to combine.

Try it in a cocktail with brandy and lemon juice; New Zealanders like it with Midori melon liqueur and tequila (called a Flaming Ho); great stirred into soda water. See Make It Your Own on pages 196–197 for unique flavor combinations and ingredients you can use to customize your own flavor.

MAKE IT YOUR OWN

Once you've mastered the basic recipes, become daring and develop your own. Start with a basic recipe, and then pick an herb, a spice, or an alcohol to add or substitute. The flavor chart below outlines my personal favorites, but feel free to create your own and go wild.

Aviation Pickled Pears
Instead of crème de violette liqueur and juniper berries, substitute:
brandy (1 ounce)
Champagne (1 cup)
Chartreuse (½ ounce)
Chianti (1 cup)
Pinot Noir (1 cup)

Pickled Strawberries
Instead of lemongrass and hibiscus, substitute:
coriander (2 teaspoons) and port (1 ounce)
Thai basil (2 tablespoons) and tequila
    (1 ounce)
nutmeg (2 teaspoons) and Kirsch (1 ounce)
sage (2 tablespoons, fresh) and Shiraz wine
    (1 cup)

Pickled Watermelon Rind
Add 1 or 2 of the following:
bay leaf (3 leaves, fresh)
cloves (2 teaspoons, ground)
ginger (2 tablespoons, fresh)
basil (2 tablespoons, fresh)

Pickled Blueberries
Instead of garlic and caraway, substitute:
honey (2 ounces) and hazelnuts (¼ cup)

tequila (1 ounce) and sea salt (¼ teaspoon)
rosemary (6 sprigs, fresh) and bay leaf
    (3 leaves, fresh)

Moroccan Preserved Lemons
Add 1 or 2 of the following:
orange zest and juice, blood or Seville
    (¼ cup)
pink peppercorns (1 teaspoon, ground)
cloves (1 teaspoon)
rosemary (6 sprigs, fresh)
jalapeño peppers (2 tablespoons, fresh)
ginger (2 tablespoons, fresh)

Etruscan Preserved Figs
Add 1 or 2 of the following:
peppercorns, Tellicherry (2 teaspoons,
    ground)
sea salt, gray (½ teaspoon)
rosemary (6 sprigs, fresh)
bay leaf (3 leaves, fresh)
Vin Santo wine (2 ounces)

Candied Citrus Peel
Try adding or substituting Rangpur limes or Bergamot oranges, or roll the peel in sugar flavored with vanilla bean, chili powder, or mole.

Pop's Sour Cherry Liqueur

Add 1 or more of the following:

*lemon zest (½ teaspoon) and lemon thyme
(2 tablespoons, fresh)*

*cinnamon (1 teaspoon, ground) and grade C
maple syrup (4 ounces)*

*whole anise (2 teaspoons) and whole cloves
(2 teaspoons)*

Lavender and Grapefruit Syrup

Try adding or substituting for the
lavender 1 ounce honey; or 1 teaspoon
cloves, sea salt or Kaffir lime leaf; or 6
sprigs rosemary; or 1 vanilla bean.

Ginger Syrup

Try adding 1 ounce tequila; or 1 teaspoon
cloves, sea salt, or cinnamon bark; or 2
tablespoons lime zest; or 1 vanilla bean.

Tart Attack Shrub

Try adding 1 teaspoon cloves, rosemary,
thyme, or chamomile flowers; or 1 vanilla
bean.

Summer Plum and Sour Cherry Shrub

Try adding 1 ounce plum wine, sherry, or
brandy; or 1 teaspoon cloves or sea salt;
or 1 Kaffir lime leaf; or 6 sprigs
rosemary; or 1 vanilla bean.

8

PAIRINGS

Put some jam on it! A common question customers ask me is, "So . . . what do I eat this with?" Because of the unconventional ingredients and unique flavors in the jams, people are eager to find creative ways to use them. This chapter is devoted to providing distinctive and delicious pairing ideas for each recipe. You can add some jam to breakfast, snacks, lunch, dinner, dessert, and cocktails.

The recipes are followed by a list on pages 242–244 of unique flavor combinations and ingredients you can use to customize your own pairings.

Love Me in the Morning Heart Eggs with Grapefruit and Smoked Salt Marmalade and toast

Laena's Ginger Scones with Wild Blueberry Jam and clotted cream

Homemade Ricotta Cheese with Strawberry Balsamic Jam and toast

Bomboloni Jelly Doughnuts with 3's Company Triple-Berry Jam

Hot Fireman's Grilled Cheese with Hot Fireman's Pear Jam and fontina cheese

*I Eat Brooklyn Grilled Cheese with I Eat NYC Hot Pepper Jelly,
sharp chedder, and garlic*

*Beet It Risotto with Raspberry Rye Whiskey Jam, beets, orange zest,
and aged goat cheese*

*Easy Like Sunday Afternoon Risotto with Easy Like Sunday Morning Blueberry
Preserves, bacon, coconut milk, and maple syrup*

*Fig You Pizza with Figalicious Jam, Parmesan and Gorgonzola,
prosciutto, arugula, and truffle oil*

Grilled Rainbow Trout with Moroccan Preserved Lemons and parsley

Revolutionary Roast Chicken with Meyer Lemon Marmalade herb butter

Beer Jelly Glazed Duck with Spiced Beer Jelly, fresh oranges, and honey

*Fig and Lemon Pork Tenderloin with Ulysses's Fig Jam
and Moroccan Preserved Lemons*

Aphrodisiac Panna Cotta with Apricot Jam and a Muscat wine and honey drizzle

Wild Blueberry Trifle with Wild Blueberry Jam, mascarpone, and rum

*Sexing the Cherry Cocktail with Pop's Sour Cherry Liqueur, gin,
egg white foam, and absinthe*

*Anarchy Marmalade Manhattan cocktail with Blood Orange Marmalade,
rye whiskey, vermouth, and an Etruscan Preserved Fig*

LOVE ME IN THE MORNING HEART EGGS

| *Served on sourdough toast with Grapefruit and Smoked Salt Marmalade* |

I was on my friend Cathy's radio show, *Let's Eat In*, on the Heritage Radio Network (an awesome Internet radio station that's all about food) a few years ago with my friend Kheedim Oh from Mama O's Premium Kimchie. Cathy always asks her guests what their favorite dish is to cook for a date. The first thing that came to my mind was "breakfast." I figured if it's a good date, then the best meal is breakfast in the morning. And I knew the dish I would make: heart eggs. Growing up, my dad's go-to weekend breakfast was "heart eggs," as we called them. He cut out a heart-shaped hole in each piece of bread and then fried an egg in each hole. My sister and I were huge fans.

My friend Caroline takes the heart egg to a new level of awesome. She masterfully prepares creative, perfect, and playful meals for her lucky husband on a regular basis. This recipe is inspired by her love of a simple breakfast of fresh eggs on buttered toast with marmalade. Use the best eggs you can find and really good butter from a local source. I love Ronnybrook Farm's butter, which is made in upstate New York and sold at the Union Square farmers' market.

Makes 2 Servings

INGREDIENTS
2 pieces sourdough bread
1 tablespoon (⅛ stick) unsalted butter
2 fresh eggs
Sea salt
Freshly ground black pepper
Pinch smoked paprika
2 tablespoons Grapefruit and Smoked Salt Marmalade (page 107)

SPECIAL EQUIPMENT
1 heart-shaped cookie cutter or sharp paring knife
One 12-inch frying pan

PREP

Using a cookie cutter or sharp paring knife, cut a 2-inch heart shape out of the center of each piece of bread; reserve the heart-shaped cutouts. Warm 2 plates.

COOK

Heat a frying pan over medium heat and add the butter. Add the bread and the heart-shaped cutouts and lightly toast on medium for 1 minute. Crack an egg into the heart-shaped hole of each piece of bread and season with salt and pepper. Cook for 2 minutes, then flip. Cook for 2 more minutes for eggs that are over-easy, 2½ more minutes for over-medium, or 3 more minutes for over-hard.

SERVE

Sprinkle each egg with the smoked paprika and spread 1 tablespoon of Grapefruit and Smoked Salt Marmalade on each piece of egg-toast. Serve with the heart-shaped cutout on the side—it is perfect for dipping in the yoke.

TIPS

For a variation, poach the eggs 2 to 3 minutes, spread marmalade on the toast, and top the toast with the poached eggs; add fresh greens such as arugula, sautéed dandelion greens, or sautéed kale.

LAENA'S GINGER SCONES

| *Serve with Wild Blueberry Jam and clotted cream* |

Scones served with jam and clotted cream are a quintessential British treat. My mother is an Anglophile. She loves anything British, and would swoon over scones with clotted cream and tart berry jam. Thick, rich, and delicious with the consistency of soft butter, clotted cream is made by evaporating much of the liquid of normal cream by heating it for a long time. It should have at least 55 percent butterfat. It turns a pale yellow color topped with a deeper yellow crust. Traditionally, it was made in Devon and Cornwall, England, and served with scones or even made into ice cream.

This recipe makes real clotted cream, and there are a few precise steps that you need to follow. Also, start with raw heavy cream. The higher the fat content of the cream, the better it will taste. This recipe won't work with low-fat or ultra-pasteurized creams. If you can't find raw cream, then use whole raw milk, or if you must, find a local cream that hasn't been ultra-pasteurized.

While you can use a candy thermometer if you have one, it's not necessary. Just be vigilant as the sugar and water mixture boils, and stir frequently. When the liquid is the consistency of thin honey, it's done and ready to go. Be careful to not let it caramelize and become candy.

Serve these scones with hot black tea like the Brits would and feel fancy. Invite friends and make it a tea party.

Makes 12 Scones

INGREDIENTS

FOR THE SCONES:

2¼ cups all-purpose flour, plus more for dusting

¼ cup sugar (⅛ pound)

1 tablespoon baking powder

¼ teaspoon grated lemon peel

11 tablespoons (1⅜ sticks) chilled unsalted butter, cut into small pieces, plus more for the pan

¾ cup plus 2 tablespoons cream

½ cup diced crystallized ginger (recipe follows)

1 ounce Wild Blueberry Jam (page 60)

For the Crystallized Ginger:
1 pound fresh young ginger (around 4 cups)
4 cups granulated sugar
4 cups water
¼ teaspoon sea salt
1 cup raw sugar, for the ginger slices

For the Clotted Cream:
2 cups heavy raw cream (or raw whole milk)

Special Equipment
1 food processor
1 pastry blender or mixer
1 biscuit cutter
1 candy thermometer
1 fine-mesh sieve

PREP

For the scones:
Preheat the oven to 400°F. Lightly butter a baking sheet.

Blend the flour, sugar, baking powder, and lemon peel in a food processor or with your hands. Add the butter and cut with a pastry blender, 2 knives, or a mixer until the mixture resembles coarse meal. Transfer the mixture to a large bowl. Make a well in the center; add ¾ cup cream. Using a fork, stir until just moist. Mix in the crystallized ginger.

Transfer the dough to a floured surface and press the dough together or gently knead it until smooth (no more than 4 turns). Pat the dough into a ¾-inch-thick round; cut into 12 circles using a knife, biscuit cutter, or ½-cup measuring cup. Transfer the rounds to the prepared baking sheet, leaving 1 inch between the rounds. Brush the tops with the remaining 2 tablespoons cream.

COOK

For the scones:
Bake the scones until light golden brown, 18 to 20 minutes.

Scones can be made 1 or 2 days ahead. Cool completely. Store in an airtight container at room temperature. Rewarm before serving.

FOR THE CRYSTALLIZED GINGER:

Slice the ginger as thinly as possible using a very sharp knife; this will be easier if the ginger is young and fresh. Put the ginger slices in a nonreactive pot, cover with water, and bring to a boil over high heat. Reduce the heat and allow the ginger to simmer for 10 minutes. Drain, and repeat. Mix the granulated sugar with 4 cups water in the pot; add the salt and the ginger slices. Bring the mixture to a simmer and cook until the temperature reaches 225°F, or looks glossy and syrupy like thin honey, 5 to 10 minutes.

Remove from the heat and let stand for at least 1 hour or up to overnight. Reheat before straining, so the syrup will drain better. Strain the mixture through a fine-mesh sieve, allowing the slices to dry for 30 minutes in the strainer, and discarding or refrigerating the syrup for another use.

Toss the ginger in the raw sugar, shake off any excess sugar, and spread the ginger slices on a cooling rack on a sheet or cookie tray overnight, until they're dry. Store the pieces in a glass jar or food-safe container at room temperature; they should last for a few months.

FOR THE CLOTTED CREAM:

Preheat the oven to 180°F.

Place the heavy cream in a ceramic, cast-iron, or enamel pot, large enough so the cream is about 2 inches deep. Cover the pot and place in the center of the oven. Cook overnight, or for 8 to 10 hours, until a yellow crust has formed on top of the cream. Remove from the oven and allow the cream to cool. Place the cover back on and refrigerate overnight.

The next day, remove the thick top layer of cream (that's the clotted cream!) with a spatula and store in the refrigerator or use immediately on your scones. You can use the leftover bottom layer of loose cream as you would heavy cream—use it in desserts or soups, or add a dollop to your tea.

SERVE

Slice the scones in half and spread the clotted cream and jam on each half.

TIPS

For a variation, add fresh herbs, such as chives, parsley, and thyme instead of ginger, and serve with clotted cream and chutney, such as Tipsy Quince and Cranberry Chutney (page 122), Mango and Lime Chutney (page 125), or Brooklyn Green Tomato Chutney (page 120).

HOMEMADE RICOTTA CHEESE

| *Serve with Strawberry Balsamic Jam on fresh crusty bread* |

Sometimes you need a little something to brighten the day and get you through the afternoon. The happiest snacks are tasty and not too filling, just enough to satiate. A snack with jam is always a good way to get a little sugar boost.

Strawberry Balsamic Jam is wonderful paired with fresh ricotta, and it helps if you have fresh baked bread.

Making your own ricotta is much easier than you might imagine. And so delicious! Make extra so you can also use it in lasagna or on pasta. I highly recommend inviting friends or family over for this snack, so you can impress them with your jam- and ricotta-making skills.

Makes One Pint Jar

INGREDIENTS
3 cups whole milk
1 cup heavy cream
½ teaspoon coarse sea salt
3 tablespoons freshly squeezed lemon juice

SPECIAL EQUIPMENT
1 candy or deep-fry thermometer
1 large sieve
3 pieces fine-mesh cheesecloth

PREP
Line a sieve with a few layers of cheesecloth and place it over a large bowl so that you can catch the liquid whey.

COOK
Combine the milk, cream, and salt in a nonreactive saucepan and slowly bring to a boil over medium-high heat. Attach a candy or deep-fry thermometer to the side of the pot. Heat the milk to between 165°F and 185°F, stirring it occasionally to prevent scorching on the bottom. Add the lemon juice, then reduce the heat to low and simmer, stirring constantly, until the mixture curdles, about 2 minutes.

Pour the curds and whey through the prepared sieve and allow the mixture to drain for at least 1 hour. Draining for 1 hour will produce a soft, spreadable ricotta. Draining longer will produce a much thicker cheese, more like cream cheese. The cheese will firm up as it cools, so don't leave it draining much longer than 1 hour. You can save or discard the liquid, which is whey. Chill the ricotta, covered, in the refrigerator; it will keep for about 1 week but will taste best if eaten within the next 2 days.

SERVE

Lightly toast pieces of thick-cut sourdough bread. (If you live in New York City, I recommend Roberta's Bread made in Bushwick, Brooklyn, or Sullivan Street Bread, made by the infamous Jim Lahey. Or make your own! Try using Jim Lahey's No Kneed recipe. It's very easy for first-time bakers.) Spread the fresh ricotta on the toast and add jam, such as Strawberry Balsamic Jam (page 39).

TIPS

Please note that ultra-high-temperature pasteurized (UHT) milk does not work as well as regular pasteurized milk. It has a smaller yield, and the curds do weird things and seem to not cling as well. Most organic milk is UHT because it's made to last for a long time on the shelf. So use a local not UHT pasteurized milk (Battenkill Farm and Ronnybrook Farm sell delicious organic, non-UHT milk in New York City) if you can.

Have extra ricotta? Add it to your favorite lasagna or fresh pasta, or spread some on toast with a drizzle of honey for breakfast.

BOMBOLONI JELLY DOUGHNUTS

| Make it with 3's Company Triple-Berry Jam—these doughnuts are an Italian jam-filled treat |

Doughnuts always intimidated me until my friend Carla, a masterful pastry chef and patient demonstrator, showed me how to make them. So fun and easy! Plus you can use an interchangeable array of jam flavors in the center.

Called *bomboloni* in Tuscany and *sufganiyot* in Israel, they are incredibly popular wherever they're served. In Italy they're made with the jelly or marmalade injected through the top, but otherwise resemble their other jelly doughnut cousins. In Israel and the Orthodox neighborhoods near my house in Brooklyn, these are eaten during Hanukkah to commemorate the miracle of the Temple oil. Who doesn't love a tradition where you get to eat jelly doughnuts?

I'm not much of a baker, but I love making special treats for friends and family, especially ones that are easy to execute; these doughnuts are a great treat that can be made anytime. I love serving them at brunch with simple ham and Gruyère cheese omelets and coffee for dipping them into. They're also great to serve to kids, and healthier than the store-bought variety.

If you're making these for grown-ups with mature palates, try substituting Finger Lakes Wine Grape Jelly (page 73) or Blackberry and Lavender Jam (page 136) for the 3's Company Triple-Berry Jam. This dessert takes about two and a half hours total, with a half hour prep time, about an hour and a half inactive time as the dough rises, and then about twenty minutes to cook and cool.

Makes 12 to 18 Doughnuts

INGREDIENTS

1 envelope dry active yeast (2½ teaspoons)
1 cup lukewarm milk, plus more as needed
1 vanilla bean, split and scraped
2 tablespoons granulated sugar
4 to 4½ cups white bread flour, plus more for dusting
1 teaspoon sea salt
2 large eggs, beaten
2 tablespoons (¼ stick) unsalted butter, melted and cooled to room temperature

Vegetable oil, such as canola, for the bowl and frying
¼ cup light muscovado sugar mixed with 1 teaspoon ground cinnamon, for dusting
½ cup (4 ounces) 3's Company Triple-Berry Jam (page 41), at room temperature

SPECIAL EQUIPMENT
1 biscuit cutter or cookie cutter (3-inch diameter)
1 pastry bag with a ½-inch round tip (alternately, use a plastic ziplock bag fitted with a
    ½-inch round tip)
Stand mixer, optional

PREP

In large bowl or the bowl of a mixer, mix the yeast with 2 tablespoons of the milk, the vanilla bean seeds, and granulated sugar, and let sit until foamy, 5 to 10 minutes. Stir in 4 cups flour and the salt. Add the remaining milk to the flour.

Add the eggs and butter to the flour mixture. Mix the ingredients with a fork so they develop into a soft and flexible dough that's not too sticky. Depending on dough's consistency, add more milk or flour, if needed, 1 tablespoon at a time. Turn the dough out onto a lightly floured surface and knead until smooth and stretchy. You may prefer to do this in a mixer fitted with a dough hook, as it will take less time. Once smooth and stretchy, transfer the dough to a lightly oiled bowl, cover, and let rise until doubled in size, about 2 hours. Gently deflate the dough by punching it down. Turn out the dough onto a lightly floured surface and knead for a few seconds. With a lightly floured rolling pin, gradually roll out the dough to about ½ inch thick. As you roll the dough, let it rest occasionally for a few seconds. Cut the dough into 3-inch rounds (golf-ball size) with a lightly floured biscuit cutter or cookie cutter. Reuse the scraps to make more balls. Place the balls on lightly floured baking sheets, spacing them apart, and cover gently with a dry towel. Let rise in a warm spot until doubled in size, about 20 minutes.

Pinch off fist-size pieces of dough and form them into small balls, about the size of a gumball. Cover the balls with a towel and let sit at room temperature for 20 minutes.

COOK

Heat vegetable oil 4 inches deep in a deep fryer, deep 6- to 8-quart Dutch oven, or stainless-steel pot to 350°F.

Transfer the risen balls to the hot oil and fry, a few at a time, until golden and puffed, turning frequently, 5 to 7 minutes.

Lift the doughnuts from the oil using a slotted spoon and let drain on paper towels for a few minutes, then roll the doughnuts on a plate of the sugar-cinnamon mixture. Let cool a few minutes.

Fill a pastry bag or ziplock bag fitted with a small ½-inch round tip with 3's Company Triple-Berry Jam. Poke a small hole in each doughnut and insert the tip, piping 2 teaspoons jam into the doughnut, being careful to not insert the pastry tip too far, or the jam will shoot out the other side. Repeat with each doughnut.

SERVE

Serve immediately while still slightly warm, along with coffee or hot cocoa.

TIPS

As a variation, try adding 2 ounces orange blossom water, rum, or brandy to the initial milk mixture; or make apple cider doughnuts with spiced beer jelly or apple butter filling by substituting 1 cup apple cider and ½ cup buttermilk for the milk, and cutting the yeast and using baking soda and baking powder instead; experiment with other dry ingredients for dusting at the end, such as cocoa powder, vanilla sugar, cardamom sugar, or confectioner's sugar.

HOT FIREMAN'S GRILLED CHEESE

| Make it with fontina cheese and Hot Fireman's Pear Jam on crusty bread |

The iconic sandwich you love is not just for kids. Basic in its assembly and simply perfect in its comfort, grilled cheese is the sandwich that's as easy to put together as it is to satisfy. The classic American version, with gooey orange cheese and sliced white bread, may be what you envision, but grilled cheese can be much cooler. This recipe and the following are adult versions that use the classic sandwich as a base for the jam and jelly you've been making.

With sweet, salty, and pungent fontina cheese and a thick spread of Hot Fireman's Pear Jam on crusty bread, this sandwich wows with its fusion of sweetness and spice. You can use olive oil or butter for brushing on the bread, but olive oil will brown the bread to a nicer color.

Makes 4 Servings

INGREDIENTS

8 slices crusty sourdough bread

2 tablespoons olive oil or melted butter

½ cup (4 ounces) Hot Fireman's Pear Jam (page 65)

6 ounces sliced fontina cheese

SPECIAL EQUIPMENT

1 grill pan or panini press

PREP

Preheat a grill pan or panini press. Arrange the bread slices on a work surface and brush 1 side of each slice with the olive oil or melted butter. Turn the oiled sides of the bread face down. Spread the jam on 4 slices of the bread. Top with the fontina cheese and close the sandwiches with the remaining slices of bread.

COOK

Grill the sandwiches over moderate heat, turning once, until the bread is lightly toasted and the cheese is melted, 5 to 6 minutes.

SERVE

Transfer the sandwiches to a cutting board, halve, and serve immediately. I like to serve mine with a ramekin of hot sauce on the side to dip the sandwich into.

TIPS

As a variation, try this grilled cheese with Pickled Watermelon Rind (page 172) and Spiced Beer Jelly (page 76).

I EAT BROOKLYN GRILLED CHEESE

| *Make it with sharp Cheddar, sliced garlic, and I Eat NYC Hot Pepper Jelly* |

The grilled cheese gets hip. This recipe, like the previous one, is an adult version of the classic sandwich and another great way to incorporate all that jam and jelly you've been making.

With sharp Cheddar, a thick spread of I Eat NYC Hot Pepper Jelly, and slices of fresh garlic on crusty bread, this sandwich triumphs its fusion of sweetness and spice. I love to use Cabot's English-inspired clothbound Cheddar aged by the Cellars at Jasper Hill. It's perfect for this grown-up grilled cheese: sharp, slight nutty, and caramelized, with little nuggets of crunchy candied texture. You can use either olive oil or butter for brushing on the bread, but olive oil will brown it to a nicer shade.

Makes 4 Servings

INGREDIENTS

8 slices crusty sourdough or wheat bread
2 tablespoons olive oil or melted butter
½ cup (4 ounces) I Eat NYC Hot Pepper Jelly (page 79)
4 cloves garlic, sliced thinly
6 ounces sliced sharp Cheddar

SPECIAL EQUIPMENT
1 grill pan or panini press

PREP

Preheat a grill pan or panini press. Arrange the bread slices on a work surface and brush 1 side of each slice with the olive oil or melted butter. Turn the oiled sides of the bread face down. Spread the jelly on 4 slices of the bread. Top with the sliced garlic (1 clove per piece of bread) and the Cheddar, and close the sandwiches with the remaining slices of bread.

COOK

Grill the sandwiches over moderate heat, turning once, until the bread is lightly toasted and the cheese is melted, 5 to 6 minutes.

SERVE

Transfer the sandwiches to a cutting board, halve, and serve immediately with a glass of Brown Ale to drink and slices of crispy fall apple on the side.

TIPS

As a variation, try this grilled cheese with slices of apple.

BEET IT RISOTTO

| *Make it with Raspberry Rye Whiskey Jam, beets, orange zest, and aged goat cheese* |

Risotto is one of my favorite dishes to prepare, and I like to incorporate homemade ingredients like jam and preserved fruits. In addition to giving the risotto terrific flavor, adding berry jam makes it much more colorful and fun.

Risotto gets a bad rap as a tricky dish that requires constant stirring. When my family made it when I was growing up, my father used to command me to stir, and when I stepped away or paused, his voice would boom across the house, "Keep stirring!" I had the idea that I would ruin dinner if I didn't stir constantly, and I associated the dish with anxiety and aching arms. It wasn't until I started experimenting as an adult that I realized you don't have to stir constantly. Stir every few minutes as the liquid evaporates to prevent scorching, and the dish is easy and delicious.

This recipe won an award at the second Annual Risotto Challenge in 2009, where amateur and professional cooks competed in a benefit for Just Food, New York City's local and sustainable food think tank.

A bright magenta-colored risotto, this dish delights with tart fruit notes from the Raspberry Rye Whiskey Jam and a rich flavor from the beets and goat cheese.

Makes 4 Servings

INGREDIENTS
3 medium beets
6 cups chicken stock
1 small white onion, minced
1 tablespoon olive oil or 3 tablespoons butter
2 cups Italian short-grain rice, such as carnaroli or arborio
1½ cups dry vermouth
1 teaspoon salt
¼ teaspoon freshly ground pepper
½ cup Raspberry Rye Whiskey Jam (page 45)
½ cup aged goat cheese
1 orange, zested and juiced, reserving 1 tablespoon juice

PREP

Cook beets with water and bring to a boil over high heat. Cover and turn heat to medium-low. Cook for half an hour, or until fork-tender; let cool. When the beets are cool enough to handle, peel them, discarding the stems and root ends, then cut them into ½-inch cubes. While the beets are cooling, bring the stock to a bare simmer in a 2- to 3-quart saucepan. Keep at a bare simmer, covered.

COOK

Cook the onion in the olive oil in a wide 4- to 6-quart nonreactive pot over moderate heat, stirring occasionally, until softened, about 3 minutes. Add the rice and cook, stirring constantly, 1 minute, until the rice is coated in oil and slightly toasted.

Add the vermouth and bring to a simmer, stirring until absorbed, about 1 minute. Stir in ½ cup of the simmering stock and simmer briskly, stirring frequently, until the stock is absorbed. Continue simmering and adding stock, about ½ cup at a time, stirring frequently to prevent scorching and allowing the stock to be absorbed before adding more, until the rice is just tender and creamy looking, 18 to 22 minutes.

Stir in cubed beets, salt, and pepper; cook until heated through. Stir in the Raspberry Rye Whiskey Jam. Thin as necessary with some of the leftover stock, then stir in the goat cheese, orange zest and juice, and remove from heat.

SERVE

Divide the risotto among 4 small bowls and serve immediately with a glass of sparkling rosé, such as Juve y Camps Cava Brut Rosé Sparkling Wine NV or Schramsberg Mirabelle Brut Rosé NV, which has notes of raspberry and is a delicious wine from Napa Valley.

TIPS

Using stock instead of broth will produce a much more flavorful and rich risotto. You can find it ready-made in the grocery store, or you can make your own. Save your duck, chicken, or beef bones and veggie scraps in the freezer, then cook up a pot of stock and freeze it for future use. Nothing compares to the rich flavor. I like to give the bones a quick roast in the oven before making stock; it will make the flavor even richer.

As a variation, use Strawberry Balsamic Jam (page 39); add lemon zest and fresh raspberries; try another type of cheese, such as aged Gouda or Manchego.

EASY LIKE SUNDAY AFTERNOON RISOTTO

| Make it with Easy Like Sunday Morning Blueberry Preserves, bacon, coconut milk, and maple syrup |

A perfect risotto for breakfast or brunch, this lightly sweet variation on rice pudding provides healthy carbohydrates and rich flavor to start your day off right. This dish keeps well in the refrigerator, so feel free to double the ratios. I recommend using the best maple syrup you can find; one of my favorites is Blis, which is aged in bourbon barrels.

Makes 4 Servings

INGREDIENTS
4 strips bacon (to equal ½ cup chopped)
4 cups milk
14 ounces coconut milk (1 can)
2 tablespoons honey
1 vanilla bean, split and scraped
1 tablespoon (⅛ stick) unsalted butter
2 cups Italian short-grain rice, such as carnaroli or arborio
½ cup maple syrup
Pinch salt
½ cup Easy Like Sunday Morning Blueberry Preserves (page 95)

PREP
Chop the bacon strips into ½-inch pieces.

COOK
Heat a dry nonstick frying pan and, when hot, fry the bacon pieces until browned and crisp. Drain on paper towels and set aside.

Heat the milk, coconut milk, honey, and vanilla bean seeds and bean pod in a small nonreactive saucepan; over medium heat cook until steam starts to rise from the surface, but do not boil.

Add the butter to a 4-quart nonreactive pot and melt over medium heat. Pour in the rice and cook for 1 minute in the butter, stirring to coat grains.

Add the milk mixture 1 ladle at a time until each ladle is absorbed, stirring every minute to prevent scorching.

When the rice is just about done but still firm, add ¼ cup maple syrup and the salt. Continue adding the milk until all 6 cups are absorbed. The rice should be al dente at this stage. Add the blueberry preserves and stir well to combine. Remove from heat.

SERVE

Divide the risotto among 4 small bowls, drizzle with the remaining maple syrup, and sprinkle with the bacon pieces.

TIPS

As a variation, use soy or hemp milk instead of regular cow's milk; add orange zest and fresh blueberries; use 3's Company Triple-Berry Jam (page 41) instead of Easy Like Sunday Morning Blueberry Preserves.

FIG YOU PIZZA

| *Make it with Parmesan and Gorgonzola, Figalicious Jam, prosciutto, arugula, and truffle oil* |

Making pizza at home is a great group activity to do with friends or kids since once the dough has risen, it's a quick dish. Making your own dough allows you to control the texture and flavor, plus it's fun and therapeutic to knead dough.

Total preparation time is over an hour, allowing at least one hour for the dough to rise. Actual cooking time takes about twenty minutes.

Makes About 6 Servings

INGREDIENTS
FOR THE PIZZA CRUST:
½ teaspoon active dry yeast
¾ cup warm water
2 cups all-purpose flour, plus more for dusting
½ teaspoon kosher salt
2 tablespoons olive oil, plus 2 teaspoons for bowl

FOR THE TOPPINGS:
1 tablespoon olive oil
2 teaspoons plus ½ teaspoon kosher salt
8 tablespoons Figalicious Jam (page 68)
1 cup crumbled Gorgonzola
1 cup shaved Parmesan
Pinch freshly ground black pepper
6 ounces thinly sliced prosciutto
1 bunch arugula, washed and rinsed
½ teaspoon truffle oil
½ teaspoon balsamic vinegar

SPECIAL EQUIPMENT
1 pizza stone or rectangular sheet tray
1 pizza paddle or square of cardboard, for placing pizza in oven

PREP

FOR THE CRUST:

Sprinkle the yeast over ¾ cup warm water in a bowl.

In a large bowl, mix the flour and salt; stirring with a fork, add the 2 tablespoons olive oil in a steady drizzle. Keep stirring until it's mixed through. Pour in the yeast-water mixture and stir until combined.

Coat a separate large bowl with 2 teaspoons olive oil, then add the dough and form into a ball. Toss gently to coat the ball of dough with the olive oil, then cover the bowl with plastic wrap and allow the dough to rise for at least 1 hour, or up to a few days. I like to let it sit overnight on the counter. When the dough has risen, preheat the oven to 500°F and place the oven rack in the lowest position. If you are using a pizza stone, place it in the oven now to warm.

COOK

FOR THE TOPPINGS:

On a lightly floured surface, roll out the pizza dough as thinly as possible. Place the dough on a large baking sheet, or if you are using a pizza stone, then place the dough on a wooden pizza paddle or piece of cardboard. Drizzle the dough with the olive oil and sprinkle with 1 teaspoon salt. Spread the fig jam over the surface of the dough, leaving a ¼-inch edge bare. Sprinkle the Gorgonzola and ½ cup Parmesan on the pizza crust, covering as evenly as possible. Dust with 1 teaspoon salt and the pepper. If you are using a pizza stone, gently slide the pizza with a pizza paddle or cardboard onto the stone starting at the back, being careful to not burn yourself or scrunch the pizza. Bake the pizza until the crust is golden and the cheese is bubbly and starting to brown in spots, 10 to 15 minutes.

Remove from the oven and let rest 5 minutes. Lay the prosciutto slices over the pizza and sprinkle generously with the arugula and the remaining Parmesan shavings. Drizzle with the truffle oil and vinegar. Give a final sprinkle with the remaining ½ teaspoon salt.

SERVE

Cut the pizza into wedges or squares and serve immediately with a glass of Summer Plum and Sour Cherry Shrub (page 194).

TIPS

As a variation, try using fresh mozzarella or fontina cheese instead of Gorgonzola; add ¼ cup Moroccan Preserved Lemons (page 176), to the pizza along with the arugula and drizzle with 2 teaspoons of their brine.

GRILLED RAINBOW TROUT

| *Make it with Moroccan Preserved Lemons and parsley* |

Simple grilled fish, with some herbs and lemon, is an impeccable summer dish. I love eating outdoors at tavernas in Astoria, Queens, where they often serve whole grilled fish in this style, called *psari psito*. Picking the flesh off the bone with your fingers is a great way to eat with friends; carnal and utterly human, it brings out the hunter-gatherer in each of us. I like using wild rainbow trout, which has a mild, somewhat nutty flavor; it balances perfectly with the preserved lemons and a little parsley. Trout is a quintessential upstate New York fish, caught in the streams and rivers of the Catskill Mountains. From the mountain streams where my family would swim on summer afternoons, I used to watch, fascinated, as agile flyfisherman caught wild trout in the spring and summer, when the fish return to their river spawning ground. Closely related to the Pacific salmon, rainbow trout has a wonderful freshwater taste. If you can't get fresh wild trout, don't use farmed, as it tastes very different and is unappealing; it's fine to substitute sea bass or Pacific salmon if necessary.

Since this is a very simple recipe, each ingredient will stand out and should be chosen with extra care. I recommend using a smooth and spicy California olive oil. European olive oil is a huge business and cheaper oils are often disguised as extra-virgin olive oil. I like using California olive oil, thus supporting an American industry that's steadily growing. Plus, you can often get fresher oil that's been properly labeled—olive oil is at its peak of flavor when first pressed, and starts to deteriorate as soon as it's bottled.

Makes About 4 Servings

INGREDIENTS
4 whole wild rainbow trout (about 1 pound 3 ounces each)
¼ cup plus 2 tablespoons olive oil
Pinch sea salt
Pinch freshly ground black pepper
4 tablespoons chopped Moroccan Preserved Lemons (page 176)
1 tablespoon finely minced fresh parsley

SPECIAL EQUIPMENT
1 barbecue or grill

PREP

FOR THE FISH:

Heat a barbecue or charcoal grill until very hot.

Brush the fish with 2 tablespoons olive oil and season with salt and pepper.

COOK

Cook the fish 4 minutes on each side, until just cooked through and the flesh is no longer translucent.

SERVE

Place the fish on a serving platter and sprinkle with the preserved lemon pieces. Drizzle with ¼ cup olive oil and sprinkle with the parsley.

TIPS

As a variation, try adding chopped fresh tomatoes, Sun-Gold Tomato Jam (page 142), and garlic to the parsley, and spread on the cooked fish to serve.

REVOLUTIONARY ROAST CHICKEN

| Make it with Meyer Lemon Marmalade herb butter |

My go-to dish to serve friends is roast chicken. I like to vary the ingredients but stick to a basic method. Is there anything more comforting than roast chicken? The famous chef Thomas Keller includes it in his "final meal" wish list. Smart man.

There are a few rules to follow for a perfect roast chicken. Keep it simple, herbs are good, lemon is always a bonus, keep it moist, and keep it hot to crisp the skin. I like to start it on high heat to crisp the skin, and then turn it down to keep it moist and fall-off-the-bone tender. I like to add a little liquid such as wine or beer to keep the oven nice and moist and to give a base for the meat's juices. Oh and butter. Butter is your chicken's best friend; it makes it better, although you can use olive or canola oil instead if you prefer. A well-seasoned and tightly trussed bird is a must. The quality of your bird *does* make a difference—a free-range organic bird tastes better.

Makes About 4 Servings

INGREDIENTS

FOR THE HERB BUTTER:

½ cup (1 stick) unsalted butter, softened
1 tablespoon finely chopped fresh parsley
½ tablespoon finely chopped fresh thyme
½ tablespoon finely chopped fresh rosemary
½ tablespoon finely chopped fresh tarragon
1 tablespoon Meyer Lemon Marmalade (page 117)
Pinch sea salt
Pinch freshly ground black pepper

FOR THE CHICKEN:

1 whole chicken, 3½ to 4 pounds
Sea salt
Freshly ground black pepper
1 lemon, halved
1 medium onion, halved, reserving one half and roughly chopping the other
1 sprig fresh rosemary
5 cloves garlic

3 sprigs fresh thyme

3 tablespoons (¼ stick) unsalted butter, softened

2 large leeks

1 medium turnip

3 medium carrots

6 small fingerling potatoes

1 medium fennel bulb

¼ cup olive oil

1½ cups white wine

1 tablespoon duck fat (or butter, if you must)

Pinch Italian parsley, roughly chopped

SPECIAL EQUIPMENT

Kitchen twine

1 roasting pan

1 basting brush

PREP

FOR THE HERB BUTTER:

Combine the butter, parsley, thyme, rosemary, tarragon, Meyer Lemon Marmalade, salt, and pepper. Reserve extra for rubbing on outside.

FOR THE CHICKEN:

Preheat the oven to 450°F. Remove the giblets and neck from the cavity of the chicken. Cut off the wing tips. Remove any excess fat from the chicken's cavity by gently scooping with your fingers. Trim off any excess skin that may remain at the neck. Wash the inside of the chicken thoroughly and pat dry. Season the cavity with a pinch of salt and pepper.

Gently rub the outside of the bird with salt and pepper, making sure to season the entire surface. Put 1 lemon half, the onion half, the rosemary, 2 cloves garlic, and the thyme inside the chicken cavity.

Gently lift the skin and push the herb butter underneath, so that it spreads along the breastbone and near the legs; stick any extra butter in the cavity mouth. Rub the outside of the chicken with 1 tablespoon plain softened butter.

The final step of preparation is to truss the chicken. Trussing poultry is a good basic culinary skill to master and will result in an evenly cooked and juicy bird. Plus it makes you look cool. If you have your own technique, feel free to use it. I like to start by tucking the chicken wings under the body to give a nice steady base. Then, using about 3 feet of kitchen twine, start by positioning the chicken toward you. Even off your piece of string from a center point, so you have equal lengths. Come up underneath the tail, feed in between the two legs, and make a cross, dropping the strings down over the legs at the lowest part. Cross again under the legs, making sure to not go under the tail again. Pull your strings tight, and voilà! The tail and the legs have been pulled tight to keep the stuff inside together and make a hot closed cavity for perfect cooking. But you're not finished. Don't let go of the string, keep the tension and hold the string with your thumbs and push down, keeping the string low. With your index fingers, push down on the top of the chicken and make your third cross in front of the neck in one easy tie. Don't let go! Pull tight, then keep holding tight with the strings, turn the chicken over, rotate to the front, and tie off on the back of the neck with a tight knot. Trussed! If you're confused, remember that the goal is to tie the chicken into one tight and neat package with legs and wings close to the body.

For the vegetables:
Remove the top green section of the leeks, trim and discard the darker outer layers. Remove the root ends. Chop roughly and rinse the pieces well in cold water to remove any grit.

Peel the turnip and cut into rough wedges; peel, trim, and halve the carrots; halve the potatoes. Trim and chop the fennel. Combine the leeks, turnip, carrots, potatoes, fennel, chopped onions, and remaining 3 garlic cloves in a large bowl. Toss with the olive oil and season with salt and pepper. Spread the vegetables in a roasting pan and nestle the chicken in the center.

COOK
Pour ½ cup white wine into the pan and place the pan in the oven.

After 20 minutes, reduce the heat to 400°F. Rotate the roasting pan and baste the chicken with any accumulated juices, then rub the skin with the duck fat. Squeeze the juice from the remaining lemon half over the chicken and in the pan. Roast for another 45 minutes, until the chicken is nicely browned. To test for doneness, insert the tip of a knife into the fat part of the thigh. If the liquid that runs out is clear (not pink or red), then the bird is cooked. If it's red or pink, cook for another 5 to 10 minutes.

Remove the chicken from the oven, lift it out of the pan, and place it on a cutting board; tent with foil, allowing it to rest for 10 to 15 minutes before carving. Remove lemon and onion from cavity and discard. Place vegetables in a serving dish and keep warm.

SERVE

Place the roasting pan with its juices on the stovetop over high heat. Stir in the remaining 1 cup white wine, scraping the bottom of the pan with a spoon or spatula to dislodge the toasty brown bits. Bring to a boil and cook until reduced by half. Whisk in the remaining 1 tablespoon butter until dissolved; add the parsley, season with salt and pepper, and give one final stir to incorporate.

Remove the string and carve the chicken. Serve with the sauce and a simple side salad of greens, herbs, and a lemon, garlic, and mustard dressing.

TIPS

As a variation, try using Spiced Beer Jelly (page 76), add 2 apples to the roasted vegetables, and use apple cider instead of white wine for the liquid.

BEER JELLY GLAZED DUCK

| *Make it with Spiced Beer Jelly, fresh oranges, and honey* |

Ducks are cute, it's true, and I was reluctant to eat them when I was a kid. But then I learned how tasty they were! The lengthy cooking time in this recipe gives you a tender duck with perfectly crisped skin. I love incorporating jellies into glazes for meat and fish; they add a smooth bit of sweetness to the skin of poultry.

Duck is versatile meat and has rich flavor and diverse utility for the creative cook. The breasts are lovely sautéed or roasted; the legs can be braised to make confit, served in salads or stewed (I love duck cassoulet, a slow-cooked stew of beans and duck); after cooking a duck dish, I make a killer stock and use it in soups; the rendered fat can be used in the previous recipe for Revolutionary Roast Chicken, or added to any dish in place of fats like butter.

Makes About 4 Servings

INGREDIENTS
1 whole Long Island duck, about 5¼ pounds
Sea salt
Freshly ground black pepper
1 clove garlic
1 inch fresh ginger, roughly chopped
1 orange, halved
1 medium onion, quartered
4 sprigs fresh rosemary
¼ cup Spiced Beer Jelly (page 76)
2 tablespoons honey
2 teaspoons ground cinnamon
1 teaspoon ground cumin

SPECIAL EQUIPMENT
1 roasting rack
1 roasting pan
1 basting brush
1 fine skewer or knife

PREP

Set the rack in the middle of the oven, then preheat oven to 300°F. Rinse the duck with cold water, then pat dry with paper towels. Make sure to remove the parson's nose and the flesh immediately surrounding, as it will impart an off-flavor if left. Discard any large pieces of fat from the cavity and trim off the wing tips. Remove the neck, if there. Season the cavity with salt and pepper to taste, rub the outside with the garlic and ginger, and stuff the cavity with 1 orange half, the onion, and the rosemary. Place the Spiced Beer Jelly, honey, cinnamon, cumin, and the juice from the remaining half orange in a small pan and heat until combined. Set aside.

COOK

Pierce the duck skin and fat by inserting a fine skewer or the tip of the knife on a sharp diagonal (so only skin and fat are pierced but not the flesh) and making dozens of slits all over the duck. Place the duck, breast side up, on the roasting rack set on a roasting pan. Roast the duck for 2 hours. Increase the heat to 400°F and cook for 20 minutes. Brush the duck with the beer jelly and orange glaze and return to the oven for 20 minutes.

SERVE

Remove orange, onion, and rosemary from cavity. Carve and serve on a platter with a simple salad of arugula, apple, and orange vinaigrette on the side.

TIPS

As a variation, try substituting Purist Kumquat Marmalade (page 104) for the beer jelly.

FIG AND LEMON PORK TENDERLOIN

| Make it with Ulysses's Fig Jam and Moroccan Preserved Lemons |

For special occasions, roasting beautiful pork tenderloin is classy. I love using fig jam, which pairs well with the pork.

This recipe requires brining the tenderloin for a few hours. I like to start brining in the morning so that it's ready to go for dinnertime.

Makes About 4 Servings

INGREDIENTS

FOR THE BRINE:

10 bay leaves

2 sprigs fresh rosemary

2 sprigs fresh thyme

3 tablespoons Italian parsley

8 cloves garlic, crushed

1 tablespoon whole black peppercorns

½ cup honey

½ cup Morton's kosher salt (note: other brands will have a different salinity)

4 cups water

FOR THE PORK:

2½ pounds pork loin

1 medium fennel bulb

2 tablespoons olive oil

½ cup small cubes crusty bread

1 large clove garlic, minced

1 medium shallot, minced

1 cup Ulysses's Fig Jam (page 158)

¼ cup chicken or duck stock (make your own with a roast chicken or duck carcass from previous recipes)

½ teaspoon fresh thyme

Sea salt

Freshly ground black pepper

1 Moroccan Preserved Lemon (page 176), sliced

Special Equipment
Kitchen twine
1 roasting rack
1 roasting pan

PREP

For the brine:

Combine the bay leaves, rosemary, thyme, parsley, garlic, peppercorns, honey, kosher salt, and water in a large pot. Cover and bring to a simmer over high heat until the salt dissolves, 1 to 2 minutes. Let cool completely. I like to make it 1 day ahead and refrigerate.

Place the brine in a glass or food-safe plastic container or brine bag. Add the pork and place in the refrigerator for 4 to 8 hours. Do not leave the pork in the brine for more than 8 hours, or it will be too salty.

For the pork:

Later that day, remove the pork from the brine, rinse and pat dry; discard the brine.

Using a long sharp knife, butterfly the loin by making a horizontal lengthwise cut all the way through the center of the loin. Do not cut in half. Let the meat rest at room temperature while you prepare the stuffing.

For the stuffing:

Julienne the fennel bulb—if you don't know how to julienne, look up how-to videos online; they're very helpful.

Heat 1 tablespoon olive oil in a nonreactive sauté pan over medium heat. Add the bread cubes and cook, tossing to brown on all sides, 1 to 2 minutes. Transfer the bread to paper towels to cool and drain.

Return the pan to the heat and add the fennel. Sauté for 2 to 3 minutes until tender, then add the garlic and shallot and cook for 1 minute. Add the jam and warm it until it loosens and liquefies, about 2 minutes. Add the stock, bread cubes, and thyme, season with the salt and pepper, and stir to combine. Transfer the mixture to a bowl and allow it to cool.

COOK

Preheat the oven to 350°F. Stuff the pork tenderloin with the stuffing mixture. You may use a pastry bag if you don't like getting messy. Liberally season the pork with salt and pepper and tie the roast closed tight with kitchen twine.

Return the sauté pan to the stove and heat the remaining 1 tablespoon olive oil over medium-high heat. Heat the oil until it is very hot but not smoking, add the pork, and sear 2 to 3 minutes on each side.

Carefully transfer the pork to a roasting rack in a roasting pan, place the preserved lemon slices on top, and roast for 20 to 30 minutes, until nicely browned with an internal temperature of 135°F to 140°F. Let rest 20 to 30 minutes.

SERVE

Remove the string and cut the loin into ¼-inch-thick slices, being careful to not spill too much stuffing. Arrange on a platter and serve with a simple salad of endive, blue cheese, and walnuts.

TIPS

As a variation, try using Etruscan Preserved Figs (page 180), minced.

APHRODISIAC PANNA COTTA

| *Make it with Apricot Jam and a Muscat wine and honey drizzle* |

Making dessert for your sweetie? This will make that person love you even more. Apricots, honey, and Muscat wine are all aphrodisiacs, and a sweet creamy dessert might be all you need to ensure eternal love.

I'm not much of a baker, but I do like to serve something sweet and special at the end of a dinner party. I usually want a dessert that's quick and easy to make, and not supersweet or heavy. *Panna cotta* is perfect for this: smooth, velvety, creamy, and just a little sweet. In this recipe, Apricot Jam, Muscat dessert wine, and orange blossom honey combine in a sauce to spoon over the simple and creamy *panna cotta*. Muscat is lovely on its own as a summer dessert wine. With notes of apricot and orange blossom, its ideal in this dessert. Be sure to use a fresh, great-tasting cream if you can. It will make a huge difference to the flavor.

One envelope of gelatin is two teaspoons, but if you prefer a slightly stiffer *panna cotta,* feel free to add another teaspoon of gelatin.

This dessert takes thirty minutes to make, plus chilling time.

Makes 6 Servings

INGREDIENTS

FOR THE *PANNA COTTA:*
3 cups cream (the best quality and freshest you can find)
1 package (¼ ounce, or 2 teaspoons) unflavored gelatin
1 vanilla bean, split and scraped
½ cup sugar (¼ pound)

FOR THE SAUCE:
½ cup Apricot Jam (page 48)
1 cup Muscat dessert wine
2 tablespoons honey

SPECIAL EQUIPMENT
6 small ramekins or 4-ounce glass jars

PREP

Measure 1 cup cream in a medium nonreactive saucepan and sprinkle the gelatin over it; let rest for 5 minutes.

COOK

For the *panna cotta:*

Over low heat, cook the cream, stirring, until the gelatin dissolves completely, about 1 minute. Add the vanilla seeds to the pot along with the bean pod, sugar, and remaining 2 cups cream. Cook over medium heat, stirring, until steam begins to rise from the surface. Turn off the heat, cover, and let steep for 20 minutes. Remove the vanilla bean. Pour the mixture into the ramekins or glass jars. Chill until set, about 4 hours.

For the sauce:

While the *panna cotta* chills, simmer the Apricot Jam with the wine in a small saucepan over moderately low heat until the wine has reduced by half, about 15 minutes. Stir in the honey and simmer until thickened, about 5 more minutes; let cool.

SERVE

Serve in the ramekins, or dip the ramekins in a shallow amount of hot water for about 10 seconds, then invert onto plates. Spoon the apricot-wine syrup over each *panna cotta*.

TIPS

As a variation, try adding a few threads of saffron and some orange blossom water to the *panna cotta*; experiment with other liquors for the sauce, such as brandy, St. Germain, or a semi-dry Riesling.

WILD BLUEBERRY TRIFLE

| Make it with Wild Blueberry Jam, mascarpone, and rum |

Trifle is a classic American dessert, and conjures summer parties of yore with lemonade and balloons. This is a slightly hipper version, using mascarpone cheese, Amaretto, and rum. You can substitute nonalcoholic Ginger Syrup (page 190) for the rum if you like.

This dessert is served cold and works well for parties or potlucks where you need to prepare a dish ahead of time or the night before. You can plan ahead and make the cake portion one day, then prep the trifle the next, and serve on the third day.

Makes 6 to 8 Servings

INGREDIENTS

FOR THE SPONGE CAKE:
1 teaspoon lemon zest
1 cup sugar (½ pound), sifted
6 eggs, separated
¼ cup hot espresso (2 shots)
1 tablespoon lemon juice
1 cup cake flour, sifted
1½ teaspoons baking powder
¼ teaspoon sea salt

FOR THE BLUEBERRY SYRUP:
1 cup Wild Blueberry Jam (page 60)
1 tablespoon lemon juice
¼ cup Amaretto

FOR THE TRIFLE:
5 eggs, separated
½ cup sugar (¼ pound)
1 vanilla bean, split and scraped
9 ounces mascarpone

1 angel food or sponge cake, cut into 1 inch slices (recipe follows)
¾ cup rum
⅓ cup dried coconut, lightly toasted

SPECIAL EQUIPMENT
One 9-inch tube pan
One 8-cup serving bowl

COOK CAKE

Preheat the oven to 350°F. Stir the lemon zest into the sugar. In a large bowl, beat egg yolks until very light. Gradually beat in the sugar-zest mixture. Beat in the espresso. Allow the mixture to cool, then beat in the lemon juice. Mix the cake flour, baking powder, and salt. Gradually add the dry ingredients to the yolk mixture. Stir until combined. Grease 9-inch tube pan.

Whip the egg whites until stiff peaks form, then gently fold into the batter using a wooden spoon.

Pour the batter into the tube pan and bake for 45 minutes. Let cool before using in the trifle.

PREP TRIFLE

Bring the Wild Blueberry Jam, lemon juice, and Amaretto to a simmer in a small saucepan over medium heat. Simmer for 5 minutes, until warm and combined. Remove from the heat and cool completely.

Place the egg yolks and sugar in a medium bowl and beat until pale and creamy. Add the vanilla bean and mascarpone and beat until smooth.

Place the egg whites in a bowl and whisk or beat until soft peaks form. Gently fold the egg whites into the mascarpone mixture using a wooden spoon in two batches.

COMBINE

Lay slices of the angel food cake in a single layer in a large 8-cup serving bowl (I like using a pretty glass bowl so the layers show when it is served). Reserve 1 tablespoon of blueberry syrup. Moisten the cake with a quarter of the rum, then top with a quarter of the blueberry syrup and a quarter of the mascarpone. Repeat this layering, finishing with a layer of mascarpone. Cover and refrigerate overnight, or for at least 8 hours, to allow the flavor to develop and the cake to be infused with the syrup and rum.

SERVE

Remove the trifle from the refrigerator and drizzle with the reserved blueberry syrup and the toasted coconut. Serve immediately.

TIPS

As a variation, try using a different jam, such as Thai Me Up Jam (page 57) or Sugar Plum Fairy Jam (page 51); experiment with other dairy, such as cream instead of mascarpone.

SEXING THE CHERRY COCKTAIL

| Make it with juniper-scented gin, Pop's Sour Cherry Liqueur, absinthe, egg whites, and a dash of bitters |

This drink is a wonderful way to put your homemade Pop's Sour Cherry Liqueur to use. The name of this cocktail is an ode to Jeannette Winterson's novel *Sexing the Cherry*. If you haven't read it, I encourage drinking this cocktail while you do. It will help you enjoy Winterson's eccentric narrative—the cocktail and novel work hand in hand to defy your linear experience of time and space.

Makes 1 Cocktail

INGREDIENTS

1 piece lemon peel from Moroccan Preserved Lemons (page 176)
1½ ounces gin (preferably Hendrick's)
½ ounce Pop's Sour Cherry Liqueur (page 185)
½ ounce lemon juice
½ ounce absinthe
1 dash Angostura aromatic bitters
1 egg white

Special Equipment
1 martini glass or 8 ounce jar
1 cocktail shaker

PREP

Wipe the rim of the cocktail glass or jar with the preserved lemon peel, which will imbue the rim with a briny lemon flavor. Chill the glass or jar.

MIX

Using a cocktail shaker, shake the gin, Pop's Sour Cherry Liqueur, lemon juice, absinthe, bitters, and egg white (without ice) to produce a fluffy egg-white foam, then shake all the ingredients again *with* ice.

SERVE

Double strain the cocktail into a chilled cocktail glass or jar, and garnish with the preserved lemon peel.

TIPS

As a variation, try substituting green Chartreuse for the absinthe; or try a different gin, such as Brooklyn Distilling Company's gin, with stronger notes of juniper and herbs.

ANARCHY MARMALADE MANHATTAN

| Make it with Blood Orange Marmalade, rye whiskey, vermouth,
and an Etruscan Preserved Fig |

Ubiquitous on toast or yogurt in the morning, marmalade makes a nighttime debut. This cocktail incorporates Blood Orange Marmalade, adding sweet and tart notes, mimicking the traditional Italian vermouth and orange bitters.

Manhattans were my maternal grandparents drink of choice in their later years, after they tired of martinis. When my grandparents would visit us from South Carolina in their swanky Buick, they always brought along a vintage travel bar set so they could drink in style. My mother's forebears were tried-and-true New York WASPs who settled in Brooklyn in the late 1700s, while my father's ancestors were Irish and Italian immigrants who came to New York City in the early 1900s. This cocktail is an amalgamation of my lineage, melded into a smooth drink with rye whiskey, beloved WASP marmalade made with Italian fruit, and an Etruscan Preserved Fig for garnish.

Makes 1 Cocktail

INGREDIENTS

1 tablespoon Blood Orange Marmalade (page 111)
2 ounces rye whiskey
½ ounce Italian vermouth
2 dashes Angostura aromatic bitters
1 Etruscan Preserved Fig (page 180)

SPECIAL EQUIPMENT
1 cocktail shaker
1 rocks glass or 8 ounce jar

PREP

Fill a cocktail shaker with cracked ice. Chill the rocks glass or jar.

MIX

In the cocktail shaker, stir the Blood Orange Marmalade, rye whiskey, Italian vermouth, and the bitters with the ice. Don't shake, but gently stir to combine.

SERVE

Strain the mixture into the chilled rocks glass or jar and serve with an Etruscan Preserved Fig for garnish.

TIPS

As a variation, try substituting Pop's Sour Cherry Liqueur (page 185) for the vermouth; or try a different marmalade, such as Grapefruit and Smoked Salt Marmalade (page 107).

MAKE IT YOUR OWN

Once you've mastered the basic recipes, become daring and develop your own. Start with a basic recipe and then pick an herb, a spice, or an alcohol to add or substitute. The flavor chart below outlines my personal favorites, but feel free to create your own and go wild.

Love Me in the Morning Heart Eggs with Grapefruit and Smoked Salt Marmalade and toast
For a variation, poach eggs 2 to 3 minutes and spread marmalade on toast and top with eggs; add fresh greens, such as arugula, sautéed dandelion greens, or sautéed kale.

Laena's Ginger Scones with Wild Blueberry Jam and clotted cream
For a variation, add fresh herbs such as chives, parsley, and thyme instead of ginger and serve with Tipsy Quince and Cranberry Chutney (page 122), Mango & Lime Chutney (page 125), or Brooklyn Green Tomato Chutney (page 120).

Homemade Ricotta Cheese with Strawberry Balsamic Jam and toast
Have extra ricotta? Add it to your favorite lasagna or fresh pasta, or spread some on toast with a drizzle of honey for breakfast.

Bombolino Jelly Doughnuts with 3's Company Triple-Berry Jam and clotted cream
As a variation, try adding 2 ounces orange blossom water, rum, or brandy to the initial milk mixture; or make apple cider doughnuts with spiced beer jelly or apple butter filling by substituting 1 cup apple cider and ½ cup buttermilk for the milk, and cutting the yeast and using baking soda and baking powder instead; experiment with other dry ingredients for dusting at the end, such as cocoa powder, vanilla sugar, cardamom sugar, or confectioner's sugar.

Hot Fireman's Grilled Cheese with Hot Fireman's Pear Jam and fontina cheese
As a variation, add sage and sliced pears; or make a fontina grilled cheese with Pickled Watermelon Rind (page 172) and Spiced Beer Jelly (page 76).

I Eat Brooklyn Grilled Cheese with I Eat NYC Hot Pepper Jelly, sharp Cheddar, and garlic
As a variation, try adding avocado, tomato and fresh onion or cilantro and fresh jalapeño peppers; or make a sharp Cheddar grilled cheese with slices of apple.

Beet It Risotto with Raspberry Rye Whiskey Jam, beets, orange zest, and aged goat cheese
As a variation, use Strawberry Balsamic Jam (page 39); add lemon zest and fresh raspberries; try another type of cheese, such as aged Gouda or Manchego.

Easy Like Sunday Afternoon Risotto with Easy Like Sunday Morning Blueberry Preserves, bacon, coconut milk, and maple syrup
As a variation, use soy or hemp milk instead of regular cow's milk; add orange zest and fresh blueberries; use 3's Company Triple-Berry Jam (page 41) instead of Easy Like Sunday Morning Blueberry Preserves (page 95).

Fig You Pizza with Figalicious Jam, Parmesan and Gorgonzola, prosciutto, arugula, and truffle oil
As a variation, try using fresh mozzarella or fontina cheese instead of Gorgonzola; add ¼ cup Moroccan Preserved Lemons (page 176) to the pizza along with the arugula and drizzle with 2 teaspoons of their brine.

Grilled Rainbow Trout with Moroccan Preserved Lemons and parsley
As a variation, try adding chopped fresh tomatoes, Sun-Gold Tomato Jam (page 142), and garlic to the parsley and spread on the cooked fish to serve.

Revolutionary Roast Chicken with Meyer Lemon Marmalade herb butter
As a variation, try using Spiced Beer Jelly (page 76), add 2 apples to the roasted vegetables, and use apple cider instead of white wine for the liquid.

Beer Jelly Glazed Duck with Spiced Beer Jelly, fresh oranges, and honey
As a variation, try substituting Purist Kumquat Marmalade (page 104) for the Beer Jelly.

Fig and Lemon Pork Tenderloin with Ulysses's Fig Jam and Moroccan Preserved Lemons
As a variation, try substituting Etruscan Preserved Figs (page 180), minced.

Aphrodisiac Panna Cotta with Apricot Jam and a Muscat wine and honey drizzle
As a variation, try adding a few threads of saffron and some orange blossom water to the *panna cotta*; experiment with other liquors for the sauce, such as brandy, St. Germain, or a semidry Riesling.

Wild Blueberry Trifle with Wild Blueberry Jam, mascarpone, and rum

As a variation, try using a different jam, such as Thai Me Up Jam (page 57) or Sugar Plum Fairy Jam (page 51); experiment with other dairy, such as cream instead of mascarpone.

Sexing the Cherry Cocktail with Pop's Sour Cherry Liqueur, gin, egg white foam and absinthe

As a variation, try substituting green Chartreuse for the absinthe; or try a different gin, such as Brooklyn Distilling Company's gin, with stronger notes of juniper and herbs.

Anarchy Marmalade Manhattan Cocktail with Blood Orange Marmalade, rye whiskey, vermouth, and an Etruscan Preserved Fig

As a variation, try substituting Pop's Sour Cherry Liqueur (page 185) for the vermouth; or try a different marmalade, such as Grapefruit and Smoked Salt Marmalade (page 107).

ACKNOWLEDGMENTS

I t is with the utmost pleasure that I thank the many people who assisted me with writing this book, starting my business, and bringing me happiness. My family helped plant the first seeds of jam love in my heart by teaching me to appreciate food and challenging me to be creative in everything I pursue. My man, Ben, patiently lives with sticky jars and chaos, and continually inspires me with his generous heart and beautiful way of living life.

I could never have succeeded in my small underdog operation without my warm, courageous, and generous friends. They tasted and purchased my jams, came to markets, gave advice, worked booths, brought friends and family, wrote articles and spread the word, supporting and challenging me in all I do. In particular, I want to thank Kara Masi, who lets me teach jam classes in her home and shares her wonderful friends, animals, dinners, and jubilant outlook on life with me; Carla Perez, who let me cook alongside her at Chestnut, taught me so much about cooking and flavor, and has been such an amazingly generous friend; Allison Toepp, who supports and encourages my many pursuits, and who brings her special bright energy to everything she touches; Cathy Erway, who wrote one of the first articles about my business for *Edible Brooklyn* many years ago and always shares the many bounties of her life with me and everyone around her; Jeanne Hodesh, whose work for Greenmarket and love of food, music, and the good things in life bring a lush enchantment to all around her; Caroline Brown and Christopher Bussman, for joining me on journeys of the imagination and enthusing playful innovation; Eric Sherman, for feeding everyone, all the time and so well, and whose warmth and generosity make me so happy so often; Charlotte, whose wisdom and clairvoyance have ignited my imagination and who has been a steadfast bosom friend for more than a decade; Holly Wilson and Lorraine Smith for being early taste-testers and loyal colleagues in the evil empire; my Antarctic girl crew, who kept me alive in the darkness and continue to instigate and encourage all these years later; my sister, Emma, who I've been lucky to be stuck with as a playmate, travel companion, and great friend; and finally, I want to thank my godfather, Scott, who has always believed in me and taught me about unconditional love, and his belief has made successes possible, failures passable, tragedies healable, and the texture of dreams corporeal.

Thanks to my agent, Marc Gerald, who helped conceive this cookbook, all the while remaining collected, cool, and wise; and my editor, Lucia Watson, and her entire brilliant team for making the magic happen. The marvelous, talented, and incredibly kind Michael Harlan Turkell took the photographs for this book and generously brought the recipes to life. He taught me tons about food photography and food styling, and made this book happen, often shooting on my deck in Williamsburg, Brooklyn, to get the right light. I'm incredibly grateful for Ben Flanner, Caroline Brown, Eric Sherman, and Maureen Post for helping with artistic direction and food styling for the photographs. I would not have had the lovely backgrounds without bowls, boards, and other props kindly loaned by Martha Bernabe, Jeanne Hodesh, and Caroline Brown.

Thanks to my staff at Anarchy in a Jar for supporting me in the madness, and teaching me new things every day. In particular, I want to thank Emma Krautheim, who started working for me early on and believed in me, spreading the jam love through her vivid, smart, and joyful countenance, and making these recipes come to fruition. I'm very lucky to have had so many magnificent people helping me.

The brilliant, spirited, and hardworking folks at markets, farms, suppliers, and organizations that make up the dazzling web of a food community in New York City are what get me up every morning and give me faith to keep making things with my hands and sharing them. I want to thank all of them, but especially Brooklyn Grange, Grow NYC, Brooklyn Brine, Mama O's Premium Kimchi, Saxelby Cheese, Heritage Foods, Roberta's, Blue Bottle Coffee, SlantShack Jerky, Mighty Quinn's, Danny Macaroons, Brooklyn Kombucha, Z Food Farms, Rappaport Sons Bottle Company, and InTouch Labels. I also want to thank all the places, both big and small, that carry my jam. The list is too long to include here, but I'm grateful to know so many compassionate and bighearted retail merchants and restaurateurs.

Without Brooklyn and its extensive network of entrepreneurs and food makers, this book and Anarchy in a Jar would not exist. Daniel and Carla, formerly at Chestnut, let me cook in their restaurant when I first began the company, and Chris and Beth have been generous landlords at my current kitchen. Anton of P&H Soda Company has been a patient kitchen-mate, and Shamus of Brooklyn Brine has offered sage advice, beer, and comradeship since the summer we started our businesses. My man, Ben, has been a sharp knife in my kitchen, a sage business adviser, and a great friend, love, and companion.

LAENA'S LIBRARY

As a former librarian, avid reader, and jam queen, I recommend the following books, if you wish to deepen your knowledge of canning, flavor, and preservation.

Bone, Eugenia. *Well-Preserved: Recipes and Techniques for Putting Up Small Batches of Seasonal Foods.* New York: Clarkson Potter Publishers, 2009. Well-written and comprehensive canning for the urban homesteader, plus excellent pairings.

DK Publishing. *The Illustrated Cook's Book of Ingredients.* London: DK Publishing, 2010. Who doesn't love a food encyclopedia?

Ferber, Christine. *Mes Confitures: The Jams and Jellies of Christine Ferber.* East Lansing: Michigan State University Press, 2002. The most exquisite jam-porn in print, with wonderful flavor combinations and romantic instructions, such as picking fruit from your orchard at dawn as the dew has just evaporated from its surface.

Kingry, Judi, and Lauren Devine, eds. *Ball Complete Book of Home Preserving: 400 Delicious and Creative Recipes for Today.* Toronto: R. Rose, 2006. This is the ultimate preserving reference, for all the traditional recipes that aren't in *Jam On.*

Krissoff, Liana. *Canning for a New Generation: Bold, Fresh Flavors for the Modern Pantry.* New York: Stewart, Tabori & Chang, 2010. Nice, simple recipes.

McGee, Harold. *On Food and Cooking: The Science and Lore of the Kitchen.* New York: Scribner, 2004. Well-written musings on cooking and food.

Norman, Jill. *Herbs & Spices: The Cook's Reference.* New York: DK Publishing, 2002. Excellent reference book of herbs and spices.

Page, Karen, and Andrew Dornenburg. *The Flavor Bible: The Essential Guide to Culinary Creativity. Based on the Wisdom of America's Most Imaginative Chefs.* New York: Little, Brown and Company, 2008; fabulous reference book of flavor.

Ruhlman, Michael. *Ratio: The Simple Codes Behind the Craft of Everyday Cooking.* New York: Scribner, 2009. A fascinating look at cooking and the craft of creating flavor and taste.

Vinton, Sherri Brooks. *Put 'em Up!: A Comprehensive Home Preserving Guide for the Creative Cook, from Drying and Freezing to Canning and Pickling.* North Adams, Mass.: Storey Pubishing, 2010. Comprehensive recipes for homesteaders, from pickling to freezing.

Zola, Émile. *The Belly of Paris.* Translated by Ernest Alfred Vizetelly. Los Angeles: Sun & Moon Press, 1996. Food politics in Paris, circa 1873, by one of the finest novelists.

SOURCES

CANNING SUPPLIES AND EQUIPMENT

These are suppliers for everything you need to make the recipes in this book: preserving pans, canning pots, jar lifters, food mills, funnels, jars and lids, thermometers, jelly bags, and much, much more. Most of these tools aren't entirely necessary, but they make canning easier and more efficient. Many local hardware stores carry Ball or Kerr jars and lids, and those are the only essential equipment you'll need to start jammin'. For homemade ricotta (page 206) and recipes without added pectin, it's useful to have a candy thermometer to monitor temperature.

National and Online

ALL SEASONS HOMESTEAD HELPERS
www.homesteadhelpers.com
They have lots of serious equipment for the homesteader (urban, suburban, or rural), such as dehydrators, food mills, sauce makers, and large pots.

CANNING PANTRY
www.canningpantry.com
Jars, funnels, jelly bags, fruit peelers and pitters, and many useful items that are recommended in this book.

LEENERS

www.leeners.com

Great source of tools for fermenting, wine making, brewing, candy making, curing meat, and other big projects that you might start working on after you become a pro canner.

LEHMANS

www.lehmans.com

High-quality Amish nonelectric tools, such as cherry pitters, food mills, and large pots for water-bath canning. Their slogan is "Being old-fashioned is always in fashion." Love it.

METRO KITCHEN

www.metrokitchen.com

Jars, funnels, jelly bags, fruit peelers and pitters, and many useful items that are recommended in this book.

SANITATION TOOLS

www.sanitationtools.com

Good source of pH strips and other tools for sanitizing.

SPECIALTY BOTTLE

www.specialtybottle.com

Good online source for syrup bottles, weird-shaped jars, and single-closure lids.

WECK

www.weckcanning.com

Beautiful jars, although slightly trickier to use and without the assurance of a pop lid like traditional Ball or Kerr jars. Wonderful if you're canning fruit for a special occasion and want an elegant presentation.

New York City

BROADWAY PANHANDLER

www.broadwaypanhandler.com

(212) 966-3434 · 65 East 8th Street, New York, NY 10003

Good Manhattan location for jars and cooking supplies.

RAPPAPORT SONS BOTTLE CO., INC.

www.rappaportbottle.com

(718) 387-0190 · 229 North 10th Street, Brooklyn, NY 11211

My favorite source for jars, lids, and bottles, plus they're incredibly cheap. This is mostly a wholesale business, but you can show up Monday through Friday, 8:30 a.m. to 4:00 p.m. and buy directly from them. If you need more than twelve jars or bottles (a case), or large gallon jars, this is the place to go. A third-generation father and son business, these guys are a hoot. They might seem gruff at first, but tell them Laena sent you.

WHISK

www.whisknyc.com

(718) 218-7230 · 231 Bedford Avenue, Brooklyn, NY 11211 and 933 Broadway, New York, NY 10010

This store has the most comprehensive collection of unique canning supplies in New York City. Nice array of jars, including beautiful Weck and vintage Mason jars. They carry Pomona's Universal Pectin, jar lifters, canning racks, funnels, and jelly bags. Not the cheapest place for jars—regular Ball or Kerr jars cost twice as much here than at a regular hardware store.

INGREDIENTS

Sources for all the ingredients called for in this book. From Kaffir lime leaf to pectin, all these online sources ship within the United States and Canada. Many will ship internationally as well.

National and Online

BALDOR FOODS

www.baldorfoods.com

Specialty foods, both fresh and dry, like pink peppercorns, Seville oranges, Meyer lemons, and more. If you're in the Northeast, you can have their fresh products delivered. They're the fruit and specialty-food distributor for most of the fancy restaurants and gourmet food shops in New York City.

CEE BEE'S CITRUS

www.ceebeescitrus.com

Heirloom citrus, and a great source for grapefruits, oranges, and tangerines from a collection of groves owned by the Burchenal family. They're friendly, low-spray, and will ship.

EAT WELL GUIDE

www.eatwellguide.org

A free online directory for anyone in search of fresh, locally grown, and sustainably produced food in the United States and Canada. The Guide's thousands of listings include family farms, restaurants, farmers' markets, grocery stores, Community Supported Agriculture (CSA) programs, U-pick orchards, and more. Users can search by location, keyword, category, or product to find good food, download customized guides, or plan a trip with the innovative mapping tool Eat Well Everywhere.

KALUSTYAN'S

www.kalustyans.com

This is one of my favorite stores in the world, with an exceptionally comprehensive collection of international ingredients. One of the few places to reliably find fresh spices like turmeric root, Kaffir lime leaf, curry leaf, and bay leaf; also has an amazing library of dried spices, including more than 30 varieties of chili peppers; great source for beans, rice, dal, nuts, and unusual condiments, like preserved lemons (see page 176).

KING ORCHARDS

www.kingorchards.com

Best source for individually quick-frozen Montmorency and Balaton Tart Cherries, unless you can get them fresh at the farmers' market in late June and early July. They ship anywhere in the United States via UPS.

LEMON LADIES ORCHARD

www.lemonladies.com

Wonderful and wacky Meyer lemon orchard in California that will ship! If you can't find Meyer lemons in your neighborhood, order them from the Lemon Ladies.

MOUNTAIN ROSE HERBS

www.mountainroseherbs.com

Amazing array of dried spices and herbs at great prices; get hibiscus flowers, chamomile flowers, pink peppercorns, cinnamon bark, Tahitian vanilla beans, and most of the dried herbs and spices called for in this book.

PENZEYS SPICES

www.penzeys.com

Good-quality spices and extracts, such as vanilla, bay leaf, and mace.

PICK YOUR OWN

www.pickyourown.com

National resource listing of pick-your-own farms in the United States.

POMONA'S UNIVERSAL PECTIN

www.pomonapectin.com

Pomona's Pectin is sugar-free, preservative free, low-methoxyl, 100 percent citrus pectin that's activated by calcium. Because it doesn't require sugar to jell, jams and jellies can be made quickly and without sugar. Each box contains 9 teaspoons of pectin and 1 teaspoon of calcium phosphate (which is mixed with 1 cup water); one box makes about four recipes in this book.

New York City

GREENMARKETS AND FARMERS' MARKETS

www.grownyc.org

(212) 788-7476

These are places where you get fruit in New York City. With 53 markets and more than 230 family farms and fishermen participating, Greenmarket is an amazing resource. Check their Web site for updates on what's in season.

JUST FOOD

www.justfood.org

(212) 645-9880 x221 · 1155 Avenue of the Americas, 3rd floor, New York, NY 10036

Connecting communities with the resources and support they need to make fresh, locally grown food accessible to all New Yorkers. Use their CSA finder to locate and join a CSA near you!

MANHATTAN FRUIT EXCHANGE

www.brooklynkitchen.com

(212) 989-2444 . 448 West 16th Street, New York, NY 10011

Located in Chelsea Market, this store has a comprehensive collection of fruit and fresh herbs: rhubarb, Meyer lemons, tarragon, figs, and much more. You can find good wholesale deals here if you buy by the case.

THE ORCHARD

www.orchardfruit.com

(718) 377-0800· 1367 Coney Island Avenue, Brooklyn, NY 11230

For exotic fruit you can't find at the Greenmarket, this is a good, high-quality source, located in the Midwood neighborhood of Brooklyn.

LAENA'S FAVORITE FRUIT FARMS

Mostly located near New York City in southeastern New York State, these farms either have stands or offer pick-your-own fruit at their farms and orchards; they are also low-spray or certified organic. All of them are worth a day trip if you live nearby.

Fishkill Farms

apples, peaches, and cherries
Fun pick-your-own farm, run by young and excited farmers.
Hopewell Junction, NY | www.fishkillfarms.com

Fix Brothers Orchards

cherries (sweet, sour, or black), peaches, and apples
They have the best sour cherries, including the rare black sour Morello cherry!
Located in a beautiful spot overlooking the Hudson River. The Morello cherries
ripen in late June and are usually gone within two days, so get on their phone or
e-mail list and go immediately when you get the call!
Hudson, NY | (518) 828-7560 | www.fixbrosfruitfarm.com

Garden of Eve Farm

vegetables, fruits, and flowers

Pick-your-own and farm stand; they also have a booth at Brooklyn's McCarren Park Farmers' Market on Saturdays.

North Fork, Long Island | www.gardenofevefarm.com

Handsome Brook Farm

raspberries and tomatoes

Franklin, NY | www.handsomebrookfarm.com

Locust Grove Fruit Farm

quince, apples, peaches, raspberries, and strawberries

Great farm in Southern New York, with farm stands at many New York City and Hudson Valley farmers' markets. One of the few farms that sells quince.

Milton, NY | www.locustgrovefruitfarm.com

Montgomery Place Orchards

heirloom fruit, amazing and rare varieties of raspberries, peaches, apples, and pears

Doug and Talea took this farm over twenty-five years ago and kept the rare heirloom trees alive.

Annandale-on-Hudson, NY | www.mporchards.com

Thompson-Finch Farm

organic strawberries and raspberries

Beautiful organic pick-your-own farm, with the best local strawberries

Ancram, NY | www.thompsonfinch.com

SEASONS OF FRUIT IN THE NORTHEAST CALENDAR

	JANUARY	FEBRUARY	MARCH	APRIL	MAY	JUNE	JULY	AUGUST	SEPTEMBER	OCTOBER	NOVEMBER	DECEMBER
Apples	Available from storage						■	■	■	■	From storage	
Blackberries								■				
Blueberries							■	■	■			
Cantaloupes								■	■			
Cherries, sweet						■	■					
Cherries, sour						black & red sours start late June	■	■				
Currants								■				
Grapes									■	■		
Peaches							■	■	■			
Pears	From storage								■	■	From storage	
Plums							Early sugar-plums		Damson plums			
Prunes								■	■			
Quince									■	■		
Strawberries						■		Ever-bearing strawberries				
Raspberries							■		■	■		
Watermelon								Starting late August		■		

CONVERSION CHARTS

LIQUID AND DRY EQUIVALENTS

Pinch or dash	1/16 teaspoon
¼ cup	4 tablespoons
⅓ cup	5 tablespoons plus 1 teaspoon
½ cup	8 tablespoons
¾ cup	12 tablespoons
1 cup	16 tablespoons
1 pound	2 cups
1 quart	4 cups
½ tablespoon	1½ teaspoons
1 tablespoon	3 teaspoons

FAHRENHEIT CELSIUS

275°F	140°C
300°F	150°C
325°F	160°C
350°F	180°C
375°F	190°C
400°F	200°C
425°F	220°C
450°F	230°C

GRANULATED SUGAR

1 packet	1 teaspoon
1 pound	2 cups
2 pounds	4 cups
4 pounds	9⅓ cups
5 pounds	11½ cups

VOLUME EQUIVALENTS

Volumes have been rounded for easier conversion

Metric	American	Imperial
1.2 milliliters	¼ teaspoon	
2.5 milliliters	½ teaspoon	
5.0 milliliters	1 teaspoon	
7.5 milliliters	½ tablespoon	
15 milliliters	1 tablespoon	
60 milliliters	¼ cup (4 tablespoons)	2 fluid ounces
75 milliliters	⅓ cup (5 tablespoons)	2.5 fluid ounces
125 milliliters	½ cup (8 tablespoons)	4 fluid ounces
150 milliliters	⅔ cup (10 tablespoons)	5 fluid ounces
175 milliliters	¾ cup (12 tablespoons)	6 fluid ounces
250 milliliters	1 cup (16 tablespoons, ½ pint)	8 fluid ounces
300 milliliters	1¼ cups	10 fluid ounces
350 milliliters	1½ cups	12 fluid ounces
500 milliliters	2 cups (1 pint)	16 fluid ounces
625 milliliters	2¼ cups	20 fluid ounces
1 liter	1 quart	32 fluid ounces

WEIGHT EQUIVALENTS

Weights have been rounded for easier conversion

American	Metric	American	Metric
¼ ounce	7 grams	9 ounces	250 grams
½ ounce	15 grams	10 ounces	300 grams
1 ounce	30 grams	11 ounces	325 grams
2 ounces	60 grams	12 ounces	350 grams
3 ounces	90 grams	13 ounces	375 grams
4 ounces	115 grams	14 ounces	400 grams
5 ounces	150 grams	15 ounces	425 grams
6 ounces	175 grams	1 pound	450 grams
7 ounces	200 grams	2 pounds	900 grams
8 ounces	225 grams	3 pounds	1.4 kilograms

INDEX